MEMO

Jonathan Lichtei

CAST

Ben/Director	Christian McKay
Barbara/Eva	Vivien Parry
Lee/Peter	Lee Haven-Jones
Olly/Isaac	Oliver Ryan
Huw/Bashar	Ifan Huw Dafydd
Dan/Felix	Daniel Hawksford
Simon/Aron	Simon Nehan

Director	Terry Hands
Designer	Martyn Bainbridge
Lighting	Terry Hands
Sound	Matthew Williams

Company Stage Manager	Jane Bullock
Deputy Stage Manager	Hazel Price

Clwyd Theatr Cymru
Thursday 2 - Saturday 25 November 2006
Dydd Iau 2 – Dydd Sadwrn 25 Tachwedd 2006

Chapter, Cardiff
Tuesday 5 – Saturday 9 December 2006
Dydd Mawrth 5 – Dydd Sadwrn 9 Rhagfyr 2006

"Some of the most consistently exciting ensemble theatre in Britain is currently being produced by Hands' Clwyd company."
*****The Guardian 2004*

Created through the vision of Clwyd County Council and its Chief Executive Haydn Rees, Theatr Clwyd was opened in 1976. Located a mile from Mold town centre the building incorporates five performance venues: The Anthony Hopkins Theatre, Emlyn Williams Theatre, Studio 2, multi-function Clwyd Room for the community, Cinema and three art galleries.

Following Local Government Reorganisation in Wales, the theatre faced closure on 1st April 1997. The new Flintshire County Council and its Leader, Tom Middlehurst, asked Terry Hands to formulate an artistic and business plan to avert this threat and take the theatre forward.

Subsequently Terry Hands accepted the post of Director on 2 May 1997 and asked Tim Baker to join him as Associate.

In 1998 the theatre won the Barclays/TMA Theatre of the Year award and in 1999 was designated a Welsh National Performing Arts Company by the Arts Council of Wales. The name was changed to Clwyd Theatr Cymru to reflect the theatre's new national remit and its new Welsh identity.

Clwyd Theatr Cymru is the home of a highly acclaimed producing company which also presents much of its work on tour throughout Wales.

"...a theatre company which has made an immense contribution to the dramatic arts in Wales"
The Western Mail

Last season the company employed over 60 Welsh actors in 8 productions and played to over 181,000 people.

Clwyd Theatr Cymru's 200 seat mobile theatre is a unique and innovative contribution to professional theatre touring within Wales. The production of **'The Way It Was' - A New Comedy About Wales in Wartime** by Tim Baker, the sixth mobile theatre tour in Spring 2006, was made possible by a £100,000 grant from the Welsh Assembly Government and sponsorship from Warwick International Group matched by equivalent funding from Arts & Business Cymru.

"...a spellbinding adaptation...beautifully sung and acted"
The Western Mail on **The Grapes of Wrath**

President/Llywydd Lord Kinnock
Chairman/Cadeirydd Derek Butler
Director/Cyfarwyddwr Terry Hands

ASSOCIATES/AELODAU CYSWLLT

Simon Armstrong	Bradley Freegard	Steven Meo	Robert Perkins
Robert Blythe	Sara Harris-Davies	Dyfrig Morris	Victoria Pugh
Philip Bretherton	Daniel Hawksford	Siwan Morris	Steffan Rhodri
Alun ap Brinley	Lynn Hunter	Simon Nehan	Catrin Rhys
John Cording	Julian Lewis Jones	Kai Owen	Oliver Ryan
Ifan Huw Dafydd	Gwyn Vaughan Jones	Vivien Parry	Owen Teale
Manon Eames	Jenny Livsey	Christian Patterson	Johnson Willis

DIRECTORS/ CYFARWYDDWYR

Tim Baker
Terry Hands
William James
Peter Rowe

DESIGNERS/ CYNLLUNWYR

Mark Bailey
Martyn Bainbridge
Nick Beadle
Timothy O'Brien

COMPOSERS/ CYFANSODDWYR

Dyfan Jones
Colin Towns

By the rivers of Babylon, there we sat and wept as we thought of Zion...How can we sing a song of the Lord in a strange land?

Psalm 137

Year 70 CE (Common Era): Jerusalem and the Temple are destroyed and the Jews are scattered across the world, creating what becomes known as the Diaspora.

7th and 8th centuries Jewish immigration into Europe is encouraged, especially merchants.

11th and 12th centuries The rise of money-based economies allows Jewish moneylenders to flourish.

1290 Edward I expels all Jews from England.
Jews first begin to settle in Berlin.

17th century Berlin Jews thrive, and banking and merchant families become some of the richest inhabitants of the city.

1880-1930 Eight new synagogues are built in Berlin.

1917 During World War I, the British government, in an attempt to encourage Russian Jews to persuade their government to remain in the war, issues the Balfour Declaration, which promises Jews a national home in Palestine if the Entente powers win.

1933-39 Under the chancellorship of Adolf Hitler, more than half of Germany's Jewish population emigrates.

1937 The Peel Commission recommends British withdrawal from Palestine and its partition into Jewish and Arab states.

1938 Kristallnacht: the persecution of Jews in Germany reaches new levels when, on this 'night of the broken glass', hundreds of synagogues are burned and thousands of Jewish homes and shops are smashed.

1939 Britain reverses the Balfour Declaration and sets a limit on Jewish immigration to the British Mandate of Palestine.

1942 At the Wannsee conference the Nazis take the decision to solve the 'Jewish problem' by mass murder. November: for the first time, reports of Jews being methodically murdered at Auschwitz reach the outside world.

1945 January: Russia's Red Army captures Auschwitz. The end of the war brings renewed demands for a Jewish homeland in Palestine.

1946 The Zionist struggle is taken up by Jewish terrorist groups such as Irgun, whose extreme elements carry out attacks in Jerusalem, culminating in the bombing of the King David Hotel, headquarters of the British civil and military administration, killing ninety people.

1947 The United Nations approves the creation of both a Jewish state and an Arab state in the British mandate of Palestine.

1948 The state of Israel is declared and accepted as a member state of the United Nations.

1949 Huge numbers of Jews make their way to Israel from around the world, resulting in a doubling of the population.

1964 The Palestine Liberation Organisation is founded in Cairo.

1972 Massacre of the Israeli team at the Munich Olympics by the Palestinian militant group Black September.

1982 Israel invades and occupies parts of Lebanon, inspiring the founding of Hezbollah, whose publicly declared manifesto includes three goals:
- the eradication of Western imperialism in Lebanon
- the transformation of Lebanon into an Islamic state
- the complete destruction of the state of Israel.

1987 The first 'intifada' begins. Violence, riots, general strikes and civil disobedience campaigns by Palestinians spread across the West Bank and Gaza Strip. Israeli forces respond with tear gas, plastic bullets and live ammunition. After the outbreak of the intifada, Shaikh Ahmed Yassin creates Hamas.

1988 An independent state of Palestine is proclaimed by the Palestinian National Council meeting in Algiers.

1993 Oslo: Yasser Arafat (PLO) and Yitzhak Rabin (Israel) sign the Declaration of Principles on Interim Self-Government.

1994 Yitzhak Rabin, Shimon Peres and Yasser Arafat are awarded the Nobel Peace Prize.

2002 June: Israel begins construction of the West Bank Wall. Palestinian terror attacks on Israelis subsequently drop by 90%.

2004 The International Court of Justice rules (in a non-binding advisory opinion) that the West Bank Wall is illegal under international law.

2006 January: Islamic militant group Hamas wins a surprise victory in the Palestinian parliamentary elections.

Just another brick?

1945 7 May: Nazi Germany surrenders to the Allies, ending World War II in Europe. Germany is divided into four zones, each of the Allied powers of Britain, France, the United States and the Soviet Union are to be in military control of their own zone. The city of Berlin is also divided in this way.

1949 The west of Germany and West Berlin become the Federal Republic of Germany with its capital in Bonn, while the eastern parts including East Berlin become the German Democratic Republic, with Berlin as its capital.

1957 Leaving East Germany without permission from the authorities becomes a crime, punishable by three years in prison.

1961 In the early hours of Sunday 13 August, East German officials unfurl huge rolls of barbed wire across the border, and armed soldiers take up positions along it, with their backs to the west. In a matter of weeks, the barbed-wire barrier becomes a solid concrete wall.

1989 The mastermind behind the building of the Berlin Wall, Erich Honecker, is forced to resign as leader of East Germany. Within months the wall itself is dismantled.

1990 A new Germany, reunifying east and west, comes into existence.

Unforgotten
Unforgotten are
Those murdered on the border
Chiselled in stone
Their names live on
Imprinted on the memory
The image lives on

Part of a poem written by an East German border guard about colleagues killed by those trying to escape across the wall.

The Berlin Wall
1961-1989

Total border length surrounding West Berlin = 155km
Border between East and West Berlin = 43km
Concrete wall = 3.6m high, 106km long
Wire-mesh fencing = 66km
Anti-vehicle trenches = 105km
Watchtowers = 302
Bunkers = 20
People who succeeded in crossing the wall = c5000
People arrested in the border area = c3200
People killed on the wall = 192
People injured in shootings = c200

Editorial written and compiled by Elaine Peake
© John Good

IFAN HUW DAFYDD
An Associate of Clwyd Theatr Cymru, Huw was born in Llanelli. Previous work here includes: **The Crucible, Silas Marner, Rosencrantz and Guildenstern Are Dead, King Lear, Hard Times, Damwain a Hap, Rape Of The Fair Country, A Christmas Carol, Afore Night Come, Twelfth Night, Song of the Earth, Under Milk Wood** and **Hosts Of Rebecca** - completing the Alexander Cordell Trilogy.
Other theatre work includes: Traxalla in **The Indian Queen** at the Citizens' Theatre, Glasgow, Kurt in Strindberg's **Dance Of Death**, Teddy in **The Faith Healer** for Theatr Gwynedd, **Enemy for the People.**
Television appearances include: **The District Nurse, Pobol y Cwm, Rownd a Rownd, Y Glas, Y Palmant Aur, Mortimer's Law, Heartburn Hotel, Y Teulu, Llafur Cariad, Holby City, The Bench, First Degree, Foyle's War, In Deep III, Heart of Gold, Con Passionate** and **Midsommer Murders.**
Films: **The Silent Twins, The Bullion Boys, Gadael Lenin, The Proposition, Iâr Fach Yr Hâf, Coming Up Roses, The Life And Death Of Phillip Knight, 15, Cross Currents, Daddy's Girl** and **Season of Fogs.**
Radio: Bob Coves in **Station Road** (BBC Radio Wales) Caliban in **The Tempest** and Peter Shaw in **Hole** (Radio 4).

LEE HAVEN-JONES
Born in Mountain Ash, Lee graduated from the University of Exeter with a first class honours degree and won the Cameron Mackintosh Foundation Scholarship to study at the Royal Academy of Dramatic Art.
He has played at the National Theatre several times, including Lysander in **A Midsummer Night's Dream** and in Peter Hall's **Bacchai**. He appeared in the Fringe First winning production of Jonathan Lichtenstein's **The Pull of Negative Gravity** at the Traverse which subsequently transferred to New York. This is his second appearance at Clwyd Theatr Cymru, having played Danny in last year's production of **Night Must Fall**. His screen credits include: Ed Thomas' production of **Caerdydd, Love in a Cold Climate** for the BBC and **The Prince**, a short film starring Imelda Staunton.

DANIEL HAWKSFORD
An Associate of Clwyd Theatr Cymru, Daniel was born in Swansea.
Previous work here includes **Rosencrantz and Guildenstern are Dead, Romeo and Juliet** and **Troilus and Cressida**. Other theatre work includes **The Taming of the Shrew, Cymbeline, A Midsummer Night's Dream, The School of Night** and **The Tamer Tamed** all for the RSC, **The Pull of Negative Gravity** by Jonathan Lichtenstein which won a Fringe First at the Edinburgh Festival and transferred to New York, **Lunch** at the Kings Head Theatre, Islington, and **Romeo and Juliet** at the Northcott Theatre, Exeter.
TV and Film work: **Colditz** (Granada TV), **Little White Lies** (Red and Black Films) and **The Life and Times of Benvenuto Cellini** (Independent Short Film).

CHRISTIAN MCKAY
Christian McKay was born in Bury, Lancashire. He trained at RADA and, as a musician, at Chetham's School of Music, The Royal College of Music and Queensland Conservatorium in Australia. Recent work includes: Shostakovich in **Master Class** (Derby Playhouse), Monteaux in **Riot at the Rite** and **Doctors** (BBC), **Antony and Cleopatra** (Royal Shakespeare Company). Work for BBC Radio includes: **The Piano, Women in Love, Mansfield Park** and **Façade**. In 2004 Christian created the role of Orson Welles in the one-man show **Rosebud: The Lives of Orson Welles**. The play won a Fringe First and the Best of Edinburgh Award at the Edinburgh Fringe Festival before transferring to New York. Further performances included Toronto, the King's Head Theatre, London (co-produced by Steven Berkoff) and a tour of the UK. Future plans include tours of America and Australia with **Rosebud** and Christian will portray the composer Enrique Granados in the new play **Goyescas**.

SIMON NEHAN
An Associate of Clwyd Theatr Cymru, Simon was born in Llanelli and trained at the Royal Welsh College of Music and Drama.
His credits for Clwyd Theatr Cymru include: **The Grapes of Wrath, The Druid's Rest, The Mabinogion, Portrait of the Artist as a Young Dog, Silas Marner, Rape Of The Fair Country, Macbeth** and **The Rabbit**.
Other theatre credits include: **Pinocchio** (Pukka Theatre Company), **The Seagull, Kebab Shags** (Bristol Old Vic), **A Child's Christmas In Wales** (Theatr na n'Og) **The Canterbury Tales, As You Like It** (Mappa Mundi) and **Stella Time**.
Television work includes: **The Comedy Show, Nuts and Bolts** (HTV Wales), **Bay College** (2W), **Stopping Distance, The Bench, Score, Kardomha Boys, Casualty** (all for the BBC) and **Tracy Beaker the Movie of Me** (BBC and CBBC).
Radio work includes: **The Fisherwoman of Black Tar, Cool** (BBC Radio Wales) and **The Longest Day** (BBC Radio 4).

VIVIEN PARRY
Vivien is an Associate of Clwyd Theatr Cymru. She is delighted to be back, having played the leading role in **Mamma Mia** for two years in the West End. Recent theatre work includes: **The Resistible Rise of Arturo Ui** (Glasgow Citizens). Other theatre work includes: Anna in **Boston Marriage** (Bolton Octagon) and Odetta in **Sadly Solo Joe** (Greenwich), The Stepmother in **The Ash Girl - The Cinderella Story** (Birmingham Repertory Theatre), Elizabeth Proctor in **The Crucible**, Emma in **Betrayal**, Kate in **Bedroom Farce**, Lady Macbeth in **Macbeth**, Beverley in **Abigail's Party**, Morfydd in **Rape of the Fair Country, Hosts of Rebecca, Song of the Earth; A Christmas Carol, The Journey of Mary Kelly** and Sarah in **The Norman Conquests - Table Manners, Living Together** and **Round and Round the Garden** (Clwyd Theatr Cymru), **The Beggar's Opera** and **It's a Girl** (Coventry), **Just Between Ourselves, Up 'n' Under** and **Cinderella** (Northampton), **Lysistrata** (Duke of Cambridge), **Bel Ami** (Stratford East) **Bring Me Sunshine, Bring Me Smiles** (New End) and devised and performed **The Ladies Who Lunch** at the Jermyn Street Theatre, Mrs Johnstone in **Blood Brothers** (the Phoenix and Albery), Anna Regina in **Which Witch** (Piccadilly

Theatre), Miss Bell in **Fame** (Cambridge Theatre) and **I Can Get It for You Wholesale** (Barbican).

Television: **EastEnders, Lovejoy, A Separate Peace** and **Take Me Home** (BBC), **Bodyguards** (Zenith), **Medics** (Granada), **The Bill** (Thames), **About Face** (Central), **Aquilla** - series I and II for the BBC, **Llafur Cariad** (Taliesyn) and **Dirty Works** (Alomo), **Outside the Rules, Nuts and Bolts, The Bench** (BBC), **The Comedy Show** (Carlton).

Film credits include: **Ali Meek Gets a Result** (Dogme).
Radio work includes: **The Berlin Diaries, The Starving Girl of Llanfihangel, The Cube of the Rainbow, The Tales of Lady Murasaki, Touching The Linden Tree** (all for BBC Radio 4)

OLIVER RYAN
An Associate of Clwyd Theatr Cymru, Oliver was born in South Wales.
Theatre credits for Clwyd Theatr Cymru include: Billy Bibbit in **One Flew Over the Cuckoo's Nest**, Ezekiel Cheever in **The Crucible**, Rosencrantz in **Rosencrantz and Guildenstern Are Dead**, Rhys in **The Rabbit**, Oswald in **King Lear**, Curley in **Of Mice and Men**, Alan Strang in **Equus**, Jethro in **Rape of the Fair Country**, Young Scrooge in **A Christmas Carol** and Johnny

Hobnails in **Afore Night Come**. Other theatre credits includes: **Past Away** (Sgript Cymru), **Richard II** and **Coriolanus** (Almeida Theatre Company: Gainsborough Studios, New York and Tokyo), **Unprotected Sex** and **Everything Must Go** (Sherman Theatre), **Hamlet** (Birmingham Rep), **Gulp** (Made in Wales) and **Strong Family Values** - co-written with Richard Turner (Scarborough & Edinburgh Festivals).
Television credits include: **Midsomer Murders, Caerdydd, Doctors, A Harlot's Progress, High Hopes, The Bill, Life and Debt, Holby City, A Mind to Kill, The Bench, Nuts and Bolts** and **Jack of Hearts**.
Radio credits: **Mapping the Soul, A Field of Hay, The Wrong Box, Like the First Dewfall, California, Au Revoir Johnny Onions, In Parenthesis, Private Papers, Station Road, Batavia, The Day Trippers, Writing in Mist** and **Badgers in My Vest**.
Film credits: **It Could Be You, Killing Me Softly, The Losers**.

JONATHAN LICHTENSTEIN
WRITER
Jonathan is from Llandrindod Wells. His plays are **Moving the Scrolls** (2001) and **Human Rights** (2001) for BBC Radio 4. **Station** (2000) at Soho Theatre, London, **The Pull of Negative Gravity** (2004) at The Traverse, Edinburgh (Fringe First), Colchester, New York, Sydney, Florida and Dresden, and **Memory** for Clwyd Theatr Cymru.

TERRY HANDS
DIRECTOR
Founder Director of the Liverpool Everyman Theatre (now Honorary Director) former Artistic Director of The Royal Shakespeare Company (now Director Emeritus), Director Clwyd Theatr Cymru.
Over one hundred productions worldwide of theatre and opera including: Berlin, Brussels, Chicago, London, New York, Oslo, Paris, Tokyo, Vienna, Zurich. Previous productions here: **The Importance Of Being Earnest** by Oscar Wilde, **Equus** by Peter Shaffer, **A Christmas Carol** by Charles Dickens adapted by Peter Barnes, **The Journey Of Mary Kelly** by Siân Evans, **The Norman Conquests** by Alan Ayckbourn, **Twelfth Night** and **Macbeth** by William Shakespeare, **Under Milk Wood** by Dylan Thomas, **Private Lives** by Noël Coward, **King Lear** by William Shakespeare, **Bedroom Farce** by Alan Ayckbourn, **The Rabbit** by Meredydd Barker, **Rosencrantz and Guildenstern are Dead** by

Tom Stoppard, **Betrayal** by Harold Pinter, **Romeo and Juliet** by William Shakespeare, **The Four Seasons** by Arnold Wesker, **Blithe Spirit** by Noël Coward, **The Crucible** by Arthur Miller, **Pleasure and Repentance**, his own compilation of poetry and music, **One Flew Over The Cuckoo's Nest** by Dale Wasserman, **Brassed Off** written by Mark Herman and adapted by Paul Allen, **Troilus and Cressida** by William Shakespeare, **Night Must Fall** by Emlyn Williams and **A Chorus of Disapproval** by Alan Ayckbourn.

MARTYN BAINBRIDGE
DESIGNER

Martyn is an Associate of Clwyd Theatr Cymru. Martyn's previous productions for Clwyd Theatr Cymru are **An Inspector Calls, The Birthday Party, Night Must Fall, The Crucible, Under Milk Wood, Gaslight** and **The Norman Conquests - Table Manners, Living Together** and **Round And Round The Garden**.
Other theatre designs include productions of **A Little Night Music, The Birthday Party, Kes, My Cousin Rachel, Outside Edge, Pump Boys And Dinettes, Absurd Person Singular, Charley's Aunt, The Shadow Of A Gunman, I Have Been Here Before** and the national tour of **Master Forger,** (all for the Theatre Royal, Plymouth). Designs for other theatre companies include: **Measure For Measure** (Nye Theatre, Oslo), **Deathtrap**

(Northcott Theatre), **Outside Edge** (Churchill Theatre), **The Soldier's Tale** (Oxford Playhouse), **On The Razzle** (Leeds Playhouse), **Intimate Exchanges** (Northcott Theatre), **Brief Encounter** (West End). Opera designs include, most recently, **Ariadne Auf Naxos** (Garsington Opera), **The Trial** (Collegiate Theatre, London), **Die Zauberflote** (Kent Opera), **Madame Butterfly** (Phoenix Opera) **Norma and La Traviata** (Northern Ireland Opera), **La Rondine** (Royal Academy Of Music), **Le Nozze Di Figaro** (Guildhall), **Béatrice et Bénédict** (Indianopolis Opera). Martyn Bainbridge's ballet designs include: **Daphnis et Chloé** for The Royal Ballet at Covent Garden. He has also designed exhibitions and these include: **The Astronomers** (London Planetarium), **Armada 1588 - 1988** (National Martime Museum, Greenwich), **Lawrence Of Arabia** (National Portrait Gallery), **Daendels** (Rijksmuseum, Amsterdam). Martyn has designed a major permanent exhibition for **Madame Tussaud's** in Amsterdam, **Madame Tussaud Scenerama**, and a new **Chamber of Horrors for Madame Tussaud's** in London and **The Explorers' Galleries** at The National Maritime Museum.

MATTHEW WILLIAMS
SOUND DESIGNER

Matthew, known to everyone he works with as Wills, trained at Clwyd Theatr Cymru and the

School of Sound Recording, Manchester.
Other designs for Clwyd Theatr Cymru include: **The Cavalcaders, The Glass Menagerie, The Journey of Mary Kelly, Hosts of Rebecca, Of Mice and Men, Twelfth Night, Macbeth, Word for Word/Gair am Air, Damwain a Hap/Accidental Death of an Anarchist, Private Lives, The Secret, To Kill A Mockingbird, Dealer's Choice, Betrayal, Romeo and Juliet, Blithe Spirit, The Crucible, Silas Marner, Oleanna, Portrait of the Artist as a Young Dog, Hobson's Choice, Stone City Blue, The Druid's Rest, Night Must Fall, The Birthday Party** and **The Grapes of Wrath.**
Since 1996, Matthew has worked closely with Dogs D'Amour frontman, **Tyla.** He engineered/co-produced Tyla's 1997 release **Nocturnal Nomad** and has been involved in post production work for 17 of his CD releases and 2 forthcoming DVD releases. Most of these have been for the **King Outlaw/Cargo Records** labels.
Other signed bands worked for include: **Antiproduct, The Relatives** and **New Disease.** Other record labels include **Changes One Records, Stone Me Records** and **Spank Records** (which Matthew co-founded but no longer has any involvement in).
Other CD releases include 3 albums for various Welsh Male Voice Choirs and Clwyd Theatr Cymru's music from **The Alexander Cordell Trilogy** and **Brassed Off.**

CLWYD THEATR CYMRU

PRESIDENT Lord Kinnock | **CHAIRMAN** Cllr Derek Butler | **DIRECTOR** Terry Hands

CLWYD THEATR CYMRU BOARD OF GOVERNORS

Cllr John Beard
David Brierley
Margaret Bruhin
Cllr Ron Davies
Peter Edwards
Robert Ellis
Keith Evans
Cllr Helen Gambino
Cllr Robin Guest
Cllr Ron Hampson
Cllr Patrick Heesom
Alan Hewson
Cllr Hilary Isherwood
Geraint Stanley Jones
Trefor Jones
Chris Kay
Julia Lorkin
Cllr Peter MacFarlane
Cllr Billy Mullin
Nigel Petrie
Prof Michael Scott

CLWYD THEATR CYMRU COMPANY

Catrin Aaron, Stephen Ashfield, Carolyn Backhouse, Tom Bevan, Robert Blythe, Amanda Boxer, Selina Boyack, Philip Bretherton, Aaron Cass, Elizabeth Counsell, Ifan Huw Dafydd, Simon Dutton, Martin Fisher, Martin George, Charlotte Gray-Jones, Phylip Harries, Catherine Harvey, Lee Haven-Jones, Daniel Hawksford, Dennis Herdman, Emyr John, Nick Lashbrook, Rosanna Lavelle, Daniel Llewelyn Williams, Daniel Lloyd, Christian McKay, Jane Milligan, Dyfrig Morris, Simon Nehan, Tara Nelson, Wendy Parkin, Vivien Parry, Oliver Ryan, David Semark, Vikki Stone, Julia Tarnoky, Sophie Ward, Jerome Willis.

ASSOCIATE DIRECTOR
Tim Baker

GENERAL MANAGER
Julia Grime

ASSOCIATE DIRECTOR: PLAYS & TOURING
William James

DIRECTOR - NEW PLAYS PROGRAMME
Phillip Breen

CASTING
Kate Crowther

PA TO THE DIRECTORS
Melanie Jones

ASSISTANT TO GENERAL MANAGER
Alison Jagger

EDUCATION

EDUCATION PRODUCER
Anne Plenderleith

EDUCATION OFFICE CO-ORDINATOR
Nerys Edwards

EDUCATION CO-ORDINATOR
Jane Meakin

ADMINISTRATION ASSISTANT
Nikki Jones

TUTORS
Clare-Louise Edwards, Clare Howard, Tracy Reece

ASSISTANT
Michelle McKenzie

FINANCE

FINANCIAL MANAGER
Emma Sullivan

FINANCE ASSISTANTS
Sandra Almeida, Amy Hancocks

GALLERIES

GALLERY CURATOR
Jonathan Le Vay

MARKETING

MARKETING MANAGER
Ann Williams

SPONSORSHIP MANAGER
Annie Dayson

BOX OFFICE MANAGER
Marie Thorpe

PRESS OFFICER
Anthony Timothy

DEPUTY MARKETING MANAGER
Morwenna Honan

MARKETING ASSISTANT
Angharad Madog

DISTRIBUTION
Brian Swarbrick

BOX OFFICE ASSISTANTS
Jackie Griffiths, Rosemary Hughes, Karen Langford, Jan Lewis, Jean Proctor, Ann Smith, Jennifer Walters, Mary Williams

PRODUCTION

PRODUCTION MANAGER
Jim Davis

ASSISTANT PRODUCTION MANAGER
Caryl Carson

TECHNICAL & DEVELOPMENT MANAGER
Pat Nelder

TECHNICAL STAGE MANAGER
Andy Williams

DEPUTY TECHNICAL STAGE MANAGER
David Griffiths

ASSISTANT TECHNICAL STAGE MANAGERS
Paul Adams, Scott Howard, Nic Samuel

STAGE TECHNICIAN
Angel Hasted

HEAD OF WARDROBE
Deborah Knight

WARDROBE CUTTERS
Emma Aldridge, Michal Shyne

WARDROBE ASSISTANT
Alison Hartnell

COSTUME MAINTENANCE
Cath Jones, Amber Smitt

HEAD OF LX & SOUND
Keith Hemming

DEPUTY HEAD LX & SOUND
Kevin Heyes

DEPUTY (LIGHTING)
Geoff Farmer

ASSISTANT ELECTRICIANS
Gareth Hughes, Steve Roberts, Matthew Williams, Neil Williams

LX AND SOUND TECHNICIAN
Dan Armishaw

PROPERTIES
Eugenie Hardstone

PROPERTIES CARPENTER
Bob Heaton

CONSTRUCTION
Steve Eccleson, Tom Parsons, John Wynne-Eyton

SCENIC ARTIST
Mike Jones

WIG MISTRESS
Denny Evans

THEATRE MANAGEMENT

THEATRE MANAGER
Ian Archer

BUILDING SERVICES MANAGER
Jim Scarratt

HOUSE MANAGER
Marion Wright

HEAD USHER/RELIEF HOUSE MANAGER
Elena Vedovotto

SHOP MANAGER
Wendy Dawson

RECEPTIONISTS/BOOKSHOP
Carol Edwards, Elaine Godwin, Nerys Jones, Carol Parsonage, Sue Yates

ACTING CLEANING SUPERVISOR
Mark Sandham

CLEANERS
Irene Hodgkinson, Lorraine Jones, Tara Pritchard, Patricia Williams, Mathew Williams

SALES ASSISTANTS
Liz Gamble, Clare James, Luisa Sciarillo

BAR MANAGER
Salv Vena

RESTAURANT MANAGER
Rhian Walls

DEPUTY RESTAURANT MANAGER
Nicola Wyatt

PROJECTIONIST
Mike Roberts

STAGE MANAGEMENT

COMPANY STAGE MANAGERS
Jane Bullock, Helen Drew, Bethan Mair Hughes, Damian Hutchinson

DEPUTY STAGE MANAGERS
Jonathan Ennis, Sarah Gentle, Hazel Price, Edward Salt

ASSISTANT STAGE MANAGERS
Tracey Booth, Robin Smith

STAGE MANAGEMENT PLACEMENT
Gillian Lewis

ADDITIONAL STAFF FOR MEMORY

PRODUCTION MANAGER
Caryl Carson

SCENERY BUILT IN
the CTC workshop

WARDROBE SUPERVISOR
Jacquie Davies

COSTUME MAKERS
Lois Edmunds, Bridie Przibram, Ruth Turnbull

DRESSERS
Lesley Huckstepp, Amber Smit

ADDITIONAL STAGE MANAGEMENT
Tracey Booth

PRODUCTION PHOTOGRAPHY
Manuel Harlan

MEMORY

Jonathan Lichtenstein

For Hans

With thanks to Terry Hands

A reading of an earlier draft of *Memory, Just Green Fields*, was given on 10 March 2006 at Mercury Theatre Studio in Colchester by Real Circumstance Theatre Company with the following cast:

BEN — Ben Livingstone
BARBARA — Barbara Peirson
LEE — Lee Haven Jones
FELIX / BASHAR — Toby Sawyer
ISAAC / ARON — Charlie Walker-Wise

Director   Dan Sherer
Producer   Anna Bewick

Characters

BEN, *the Director*

BARBARA *plays* EVA

LEE *plays* PETER

OLLY *plays* ISAAC

HUW *plays* BASHAR

DAN *plays* FELIX

SIMON *plays* ARON

This text went to press before the end of rehearsals so will differ from the play as performed.

Opening

The rehearsal room.

BEN *plays the piano.*

BARBARA *enters, listens.*

BARBARA. It's beautiful.

BEN. Bach had two keyboards on the one harpsichord which made the variations a bit easier.

He plays again.

BARBARA. What are we doing today?

BEN. The first meeting between Peter and Eva, the first allotment scene and the memory scene.

BARBARA. Why did you change the memory scene? I read it last night. Now it's got nothing to do with the Wall.

BEN. It's got everything to do with the Wall.

BARBARA. I phoned you last night. Three times.

BEN. I was out.

LEE *enters.*

LEE. Hi Ben.

BEN. Morning.

LEE. Hi.

LEE *and* BARBARA *kiss.*

BARBARA. Did you get home okay last night?

LEE. Yeah . . . a bit late though, you know how it is.

BARBARA. You looked happy.

LEE. What?

BARBARA. You looked happy!

LEE. I was . . . so what are we doing today?

BARBARA. The allotment and the first meeting with Peter and Eva.

BEN. And the memory scene.

BARBARA. And the new memory scene.

LEE. Sounds good to me.

> BEN *carries on practising.* LEE *gets ready.* BARBARA *picks up her script.*

BARBARA. You are in.

> *Beat.*

> You are wet.

> *Beat.*

> You are wet.

> *Beat.*

> I heard it, incredible.

> BARBARA *marks her script.*

> You are in. You are wet. You are wet. I heard it, incredible. It's awkward.

LEE. So?

BARBARA. Have you looked at the rewrites of the Memory scene?

LEE. Not really.

BARBARA. I like all the Bethlehem stuff – needs developing, but this story about the two boys in the nineteen thirties . . .

LEE. I like what you're doing.

BARBARA. You do?

LEE. Yes I do, it's very moving.

BARBARA. Thank you, that's kind.

LEE. No problem.

SIMON *enters.*

SIMON. Any tea on the go?

BEN. Always tea.

SIMON. Drink of the gods, everyone knows that. Anyone else?

LEE. I'll have one.

BARBARA. Me too.

SIMON. One of those herbal things, I suppose.

BARBARA. They're by the kettle.

SIMON. What about you, Ben?

BEN. I'll make a coffee later.

SIMON. Thought you might. Did you get the biscuits, Lee?

LEE. Oh god, sorry, completely forgot.

SIMON. Because you were out of your tiny mind last night, that's why.

LEE. You had an early night as far as I remember.

SIMON. I'm a professional. So who was it?

LEE. Friend from college.

SIMON. Oh yeah?

LEE. Just make the tea, will you?

SIMON. I want to know every detail later. (*He begins to make the tea.* HUW *enters.*)

Tea, Huw?

HUW. Thanks. Anyone see the news last night?

BEN. I did.

HUW. It was very upsetting. Why can't they just sit down and talk to each other and sort it out? And what they show on the news now is obscene.

BEN. Pornographic.

BARBARA. Look Ben, I just don't want to get this ending wrong.

BEN. You won't, trust me.

BARBARA. But you've changed things.

BEN. I've developed them.

HUW. Perhaps they need to show us all those pictures to make us notice.

BARBARA. Why have you put such an emphasis on the two boys?

BEN. Because it happened, it actually happened.

BARBARA. It's in the past. What's happening now is more important.

BEN. What's happening now is because of the past.

BARBARA. Olly's worried about the rewrites too.

BEN. Is he?

BARBARA. He's going to mention it when he comes in.

BEN. If he comes in – he's late.

BARBARA. It's past.

BEN. The recovery of memory is a present-day activity. It's not the past. Memory occurs in the present, memory must live in the present and it must be truthful.

OLLY *enters, speaking on his mobile.*

OLLY. Yeah . . . absolutely . . . but that's what it's like . . . all the time, I mean complaining's complaining, you know, but when my head's between her legs and she's still complaining about the state of the kitchen . . . Yeah, it does . . . you lose confidence . . . it feels . . . you know, worse . . . look, got to go . . . (*He hangs up.*) Morning, everyone.

BEN. We'll start then.

OLLY. Sorry, am I late?

BEN. Yes.

OLLY. Bloody parking; you know what it's like.

BEN. I want to start.

OLLY. That car costs me a bloody fortune.

SIMON. What's wrong with it this time?

BEN. Okay, everyone.

OLLY. Failed its MOT. Couldn't believe it, it's only just been serviced.

LEE. What do you expect if you buy an old Porsche? You'd be better off with a normal car.

OLLY. What, you mean like a Ford?

SIMON. Mine's very economical. Tea?

OLLY. One heaped teaspoon.

BEN. From the top. If you don't mind.

SIMON. Be right there.

OLLY. The first scene?

BEN. We're doing a kind of run.

SIMON. What are we doing?

BEN. The Eva/Peter first scene, the allotment scene and the memory scene.

OLLY. I wanted to talk to you about those rewrites.

BEN. Later, Olly.

LEE. So, what's wrong with it?

OLLY. It's the bloody steering rack. Costs hundreds to fix. And they talk to you like it's your fault, like I've done too much steering. Oh sorry, mate, I suppose I should just drive in a straight line, should I, so I can save wear and tear on the rack and pinion.

BEN. Olly, could you please do me a favour and leave your car outside?

OLLY. I said to the old boy there, you don't drive nineteen seventy-eight nine-elevens in a straight line. They're built for fucking cornering. Anyone got change for a twenty? I parked on a meter.

SIMON. That's more than I spend on my car in a week.

BEN. Come on, Olly.

BARBARA. I want to talk about the new ending.

BEN. Please.

BARBARA. It's too much.

OLLY. I'll need to feed the meter in, let me see, fifty-six minutes.

SIMON. Have you seen this today?

SIMON *holds the newspaper up.*

BARBARA. More about Israel?

SIMON. No, Swansea. They're getting a new skate park ten years too late for me. Look at the half pipes . . . mega . . . and the grinding rail . . .

BEN. Stand by, everybody.

SIMON. I campaigned for that years ago.

LEE. Campaigned?

SIMON. I signed a petition.

OLLY. So will that be okay, Ben?

BEN. What?

OLLY. The meter, I need to feed it in fifty-five and three-quarter minutes. I don't want a fine.

BEN. I don't care about your meter, I don't care about your fine, I don't care if you're towed away. I want to start.

OLLY. It's a nineteen seventy-eight Porsche.

BARBARA. Where's Dan?

BEN. He's not called for another ten minutes.

OLLY. I have a problem with some of your rewrites.

BEN. This is not the time.

OLLY. They totally alter the play.

BARBARA. We're only trying to help.

BEN. Why are you both stalling? What are you both frightened of?

OLLY. Parking fines.

HUW. I'd like to rehearse, actually.

SIMON. I wouldn't mind.

LEE. Let's get on.

BEN. Thanks?

BARBARA. We'll talk about it later.

Beat.

BEN. Let's start then. *Memory.* It's raining. It's Eva's flat. It's East Berlin. It's nineteen ninety. Eva is seventy-eight.

BARBARA. She was seventy-five in the last draft.

BEN. Well, she's seventy-eight now.

Scene One

BEN. Nineteen ninety. Peter arrives at Eva's flat.

BEN *walks to the piano and starts to play the Aria from the Bach Goldberg variations. He stops abruptly in the middle.*

LEE (*as* PETER) *knocks on the door of* EVA*'s flat.*

BARBARA (*as* EVA) *stands.*

PETER. Eva.

EVA *does not move.*

It's good to see you.

An acre of space between them.

I am Peter.

EVA *stares.*

I've come. I'm here.

EVA *stares.*

I wrote a card. Look, if it's not a good time . . . Maybe later.
The rain. Can I come in?

EVA. You are in.

PETER. Thank you. Yes, I am.

EVA. You're wet.

PETER. The rain's heavy.

EVA. I heard it.

PETER. The sky opened.

EVA. Yes.

PETER. It was incredible.

EVA. Incredible?

PETER. Well, cleansing.

EVA. You don't look very clean.

Beat.

PETER. I spent hours looking for your flat.

EVA. You should have had a map.

PETER. I did. It fell apart in the rain. (*Beat.*) You look like
your pictures.

EVA. Do I?

PETER. I brought you a present.

EVA. What is it?

PETER (*hanging up his coat*). It's a piece of the Wall. The
Berlin Wall.

He holds up a small piece of the Berlin Wall.

EVA. What about it?

PETER. History. It kept us apart.

EVA. It has.

Pause. PETER *picks up the photograph of the two boys.*

PETER. Are these the two boys? The ones you saved? Tell me about them.

EVA. There is nothing you don't know.

PETER. You were very brave.

EVA. Put it back.

She takes the picture, looks at it and then replaces it. Pause.

PETER. Do you still play?

EVA. No. Let me see that.

PETER. What?

EVA. The piece of Wall.

PETER *hands her the piece of Wall.*

How do I know this is the real Wall? No writing. No blood.

PETER. There, look – a bullet hole.

EVA. Maybe . . . .

She gives it back. Beat. He walks over to the typewriter.

PETER. So this is what my grandfather typed on?

EVA. I suppose he did.

PETER. It's so old.

EVA. There's nothing wrong with it.

PETER *types.*

PETER (*reading as he types*). I am in Berlin. (*He lifts out the paper and looks at it.*) The type's wonky.

EVA. Wonky, what is this wonky?

PETER. Bent, crooked, not even. (*Pause.*) I've wanted to come for years.

EVA. Nobody else has.

PETER. It's complicated getting here.

EVA. But now the Wall is down you are here.

PETER. Yes. It's good.

Beat.

EVA. You are small.

PETER. Small?

EVA. Smaller than your pictures.

PETER. I'm average, the national average actually.

EVA. Men must be smaller in Britain.

PETER. Possibly.

EVA. There are many differences.

Beat.

PETER. I washed dishes to pay for the fare to get here.

EVA. You're a student.

PETER. Not any more.

EVA. A music student.

PETER. No. I finished.

EVA. You finished?

PETER. I stopped.

EVA. I don't understand.

PETER. I failed. I had to leave.

Beat.

EVA. You wash dishes to see me?

PETER. It took me a while. It's expensive to get here. When I came through the checkpoint there were soldiers everywhere.

Some were standing on a bridge with machine guns. And big dogs. Alsatians. Why are they still there now when everyone can just go straight through?

Silence.

EVA. I too have washed dishes.

PETER. Have you?

EVA. I did not like it.

Pause.

PETER. I didn't think it would be like this.

EVA. What?

PETER. Our meeting.

EVA. What did you expect?

PETER. I hear Bach in my mind.

EVA. Bach? Play me some.

PETER *walks to the piano and opens it.*

BEN *starts to play the Aria from the Goldberg Variations. He stops midway through.*

PETER. My playing is not good.

EVA. No.

LEE. That's because I'm not playing.

BEN. Lee.

LEE. I teach the fucking piano, Ben.

BEN. Can we go back, please?

LEE. We went through this before.

BEN. Teaching and playing are not the same thing.

BEN *starts to play again, then stops midway.*

PETER. My playing is not good.

EVA. No. (*Beat.*) I like to hear it. Carry on.

PETER. I can't.

EVA. Why not?

PETER. I don't know what happens. I lose the pulse and then I stop. It's why I failed.

EVA. But to stop halfway; are you ill?

PETER. No.

EVA. You must be. Your head stops your playing, yes? Then the illness is in your head.

PETER. I hate it.

EVA. Again. The aria.

BEN *plays again, then stops.*

Don't stop! Again. Again.

BEN *plays again and then stops.*

Why don't you play?

Pause.

PETER. Can I hold you?

EVA. No.

PETER. Please. You were dancing earlier on.

EVA. I was not.

PETER. I just saw you, you were swaying to the music with your eyes closed.

EVA. That was not dancing, that was old age.

PETER. I want you to dance with me, like you were just doing.

EVA. No. No. Don't keep asking me.

PETER. What are you frightened of?

EVA. I just don't want to dance, that's all; I can't dance.

PETER. When I heard you were ill I had to come and see you.

EVA. It's nothing.

PETER. I needed to see you before you . . .

EVA. Say it.

He doesn't.

PETER. I needed to see you, that's all.

EVA. So now you have. And as you can see it's not such a good time for me.

PETER. It must be difficult for you on your own.

EVA. I like being on my own.

PETER. You'll need help.

EVA. There are many things that are worse.

PETER. My father has told me things.

EVA. What things did he tell you?

PETER. How you saved those boys by lying on top of them when you were at the station. You were unbelievably brave. And you say you see them still?

EVA. They write to me. Elie writes often. Joshua not so much.

PETER. When did you last see them?

EVA. What business is that of yours?

PETER. Just a question. (*Beat.*) Could I read one of their letters to you?

EVA. No, you cannot. You are making me feel uneasy. I don't like the way you look at me. Your eyes are so critical. You are nosey, my flat is small, I don't go out. You take up room. Please go.

PETER. On the phone you said you were pleased I was coming.

EVA. I was just being polite.

PETER. I've come a long way. It's late. There's nowhere to go, it's pouring with rain.

EVA. You said you liked the rain.

PETER. I don't know Berlin, I don't speak German.

EVA. You speak no German? You shouldn't have come. Go. Quickly.

PETER *picks up his bag and goes to the door.*

PETER. There isn't long for you. Make peace with the past, all that it holds for you; don't drag it into the next world.

EVA. There's no next world. Now get out.

PETER. As you wish.

EVA. I have thought of you every day of my life. Since you were born I have wanted to touch you and to hold you in my arms. I have wished to be with you; with your brothers and sisters; to sit around a table in your company; to speak to you, to stroke your hair.

The door blows open. The rain is heard outside.

No visit. No call. No card. No word. Nothing. I sit at an empty table. Alone. None of you.

PETER *walks towards* EVA.

PETER. I was frightened of you.

EVA. Why?

PETER. You're German.

They face each other. EVA *slaps him.*

BEN. Again.

EVA *slaps him again.*

Again.

EVA *slaps him again.*

Again.

EVA *slaps him again.*

Hang on, everyone. Where's Dan?

HUW. You gave him a later call.

BEN. Not this late.

BARBARA. You all right?

LEE. Stings a bit but I'm fine.

BARBARA. God, it makes you stiff playing seventy-five.

BEN. Seventy-eight.

BARBARA. Seventy-eight!

LEE. Just don't do it too near my ear, okay? I once had a burst eardrum. It hurts.

BARBARA. Oh Lee, I'm so sorry.

LEE. Maybe you should hit me with your stick.

Noise.

SIMON (*standing at the window*). Look at this.

LEE. Thank God it's outside. I thought it was my ear.

OLLY. Ben?

BARBARA (*looking out of window*). What is it?

OLLY (*holding up jacket*). I found this.

BARBARA. It's enormous.

HUW (*reading paper*). Says here 'Knocking buildings down is more profitable than building them.'

SIMON. Bollocks.

HUW. That's what it says.

SIMON. If that were true we'd be in a desert.

HUW. When were you last in Lebanon?

OLLY. It's a bit big. I know.

BARBARA. It's like a dinosaur.

BEN. Where's Dan?

LEE. We can't work anyway with this going on.

BEN. We'll do the first Bethlehem scene.

LEE. And the noise?

BEN. We'll use it.

Scene Two

BEN. Bethlehem. Now. Two thousand and six.

ISAAC (*played by* OLLY). Mr Al Bashar?

> BASHAR, *played by* HUW, *is sweeping the floor.*

> I've come. We're here. Mr Al Bashar. We're here. Mr Al Bashar?

> BASHAR *carries on sweeping.*

> Why are you doing that?

BASHAR. What?

ISAAC. Why are you doing that?

BASHAR. What?

ISAAC. Sweeping up.

BASHAR. I can't hear you.

ISAAC. Stop sweeping.

BASHAR. Stop the noise.

> *He stops sweeping and then starts to clean the table.*

ISAAC. What?

BASHAR. Stop the noise.

ISAAC. I can't.

> BASHAR *is on the ground, sweeping up the dirt. The following in dumb show.*

> Now what are you doing?

BASHAR. Stop the noise.

ISAAC. What?

BASHAR. Stop it.

ISAAC. I told you I can't. You stop cleaning.

BASHAR. Stop the noise.

ISAAC. Get off your hands and knees.

End of dumb show. BASHAR *stands. Noise stops.*

We wrote you letters. You received them?

BASHAR. Yes, yes I did.

ISAAC. All of them?

BASHAR. How would I know?

ISAAC. We sent you six altogether, including the one you must sign for.

BASHAR. And the yellow form you left under the stone outside my door.

ISAAC. And the one you sign for, did you sign?

BASHAR. Yes, I signed for one.

ISAAC. And the verbal warnings?

BASHAR. Yes.

ISAAC. So you know the date today is the one.

BASHAR. Yes, I do.

ISAAC. But you are still here?

BASHAR. I am.

ISAAC. You shouldn't be.

BEN. Stop there, can you, Olly?

OLLY. Sure.

BEN. Look, he's not guilty and he's not aggressive, okay? He's bored; he wants it done quickly. You're playing him as though he cares, he doesn't. It's his job.

OLLY. From the top?

BEN. No. From the silence.

BASHAR *stands.*

ISAAC. We wrote you letters. You received them?

BASHAR. Yes, yes I did.

ISAAC. All of them?

BASHAR. How would I know?

ISAAC. We sent you six altogether, including the one you must sign for.

BASHAR. And the yellow form you left under the stone outside my door yesterday.

ISAAC. And the one you sign for, did you sign?

BASHAR. Yes I signed for one.

ISAAC. And the verbal warnings?

BASHAR. Yes.

ISAAC. So you know the date today is the one.

BASHAR. Yes, I do.

ISAAC. But you are still here?

BASHAR. I am.

ISAAC. You shouldn't be.

BASHAR. This is my house.

ISAAC. It is required.

BASHAR. It is mine.

ISAAC. It will still be yours. Are you the only one at home?

BASHAR. That is correct.

ISAAC. No one sleeping upstairs?

BASHAR. Upstairs?

ISAAC. Yes.

BASHAR. I don't have an upstairs.

ISAAC *checks his map.*

ISAAC. Are you sure?

BASHAR. Of course I am.

ISAAC *checks his map again.*

ISAAC. The map says you have an upstairs.

BASHAR. I was going to build an upstairs until you started on your wall. Then I thought you might pull it all down. (*Beat.*) You look like the pictures.

ISAAC. What pictures?

BASHAR. The pictures in the papers of soldiers.

ISAAC. Your Hebrew is good.

BASHAR. It has to be.

ISAAC. You live downstairs?

BASHAR. Obviously.

ISAAC. How many people?

BASHAR. Myself, my wife and three children.

ISAAC. Are they here?

BASHAR. They are staying with relatives. Your Hebrew is good too.

ISAAC. My Russian is better. (*Beat.*) The bulldozer will start again soon. They need to build this section of Wall.

BASHAR. It will pass through my house.

ISAAC. No, no, not through your house. (*He opens a case. Goes through some papers.*) Through your garden.

BASHAR. Yes, and then you will knock down my kitchen wall.

ISAAC *consults the documents.*

ISAAC. Oh yes, we will. Your kitchen wall. To keep everyone safe.

BASHAR. It does not work.

ISAAC. It works already. Your terrorists have been quiet.

BASHAR. They are not my terrorists.

ISAAC. You are like my uncle, he argues about everything.

BASHAR. And what about the rockets that go over the Wall?

ISAAC. That's not my responsibility.

BASHAR. Did you not think about rockets when you think of this Wall?

ISAAC. I didn't think of this Wall.

BASHAR. So who did?

Beat.

ISAAC. The piano.

BASHAR. You change the subject.

ISAAC. Yes. Do you play?

BASHAR. I used to.

ISAAC. Play.

BASHAR. No.

ISAAC. Then come with me.

BASHAR. No. You will pull down my house.

ISAAC. I told you we only need your garden.

BASHAR. Just my garden? I thought you were taking my house.

ISAAC. No, just your garden.

BASHAR. This is good because the document you left me under the stone said that you were pulling down part of my house because it was too close to the Wall; that it was less than eighty metres from the Wall.

ISAAC. Your house is safe. Look at the map.

ISAAC *opens the map out. They look.*

See, here, just your garden.

BASHAR. Here?

ISAAC. Yes, your house, the Wall is through the garden only.

BASHAR. This is not my house. This is my house. Here.

ISAAC *turns the map.*

ISAAC. I see. Yes. I was wrong. (*He consults the map.*) You were right. Soon we will pull down half your house.

Bloody hell.

Back to the rehearsal room.

DAN *enters carrying a large bag.*

DAN. Sorry Ben, it won't happen again.

BEN. You're late.

DAN. I was waiting outside. Didn't want to interrupt.

BEN. Everyone else gets here for the start.

DAN. You gave me a later call.

BEN. You're late for your later call.

DAN. Sorry everyone, sorry. (*Beat.*) I got these.

DAN *pulls out of his bag a large bunch of flowers.*

BARBARA. Oh, they're beautiful. They smell wonderful.

DAN. We can use them later on. Aren't they amazing? Look at these sunflowers against the eucalyptus.

BARBARA. They're fantastic. I love them. And the smell!

Scene Three

BEN. Okay. Standby. Memory one. Midnight. Moonlight.
Sound of trees. Summer. It's nineteen thirty-three. Eva is
twenty-one.

EVA *dries herself with a towel.*

SIMON, *as* ARON, *enters. He has been swimming too.*

ARON. You're fast.

EVA. It's all in the kick.

ARON. A bit of you must be mermaid.

EVA. When I swim, I swim quickly.

ARON. I wonder where Felix is now?

ARON *gazes out to the lake to see him.* EVA *joins him.*

EVA. He's not far away; The moonlight's catching his
splashes, can you see?

ARON. He must have gone out to the buoy. He said he would
when we waded in.

EVA. I wish he wasn't leaving.

ARON. I'll make coffee.

ARON *brings out the new stove.*

EVA. On your new stove?

ARON. On my new stove.

EVA. Let me see it. It's very nice, Aron, I like it very much.

ARON. You do?

EVA. It's a . . . er . . .

ARON. A stove.

EVA. It's a very nice stove. (*Calling.*) Felix! We're over here!
Felix! Isn't he amazing, he's gone right out. Felix!

ARON. I haven't been to this side of the lake before. It gets
deep so quickly. The other side slopes more gently. This
side the water's much colder.

EVA. When I swim here in early autumn it hits my chest like a hammer. Come on, Felix!

ARON. Look at the moon. What colour would you say it is?

EVA. I don't know. It's difficult to describe.

ARON. Perhaps there's no word for it.

The sound of an owl.

When I was young the night frightened me. Now I think of it as a friend.

EVA. It still scares me.

ARON. It always seems so peaceful.

DAN, *as* FELIX, *enters with a towel.*

EVA. Did you get all the way to the buoy?

FELIX. I got there and I held onto it with both hands. It's really rusty. Originally it was pale green, you can see where the paint hasn't flaked, and it must have been there for years because it's held together with nuts and bolts instead of rivets, which makes it a very old one.

EVA. We saw your splashes.

FELIX. I'm glad you called me because I went a bit further than I meant to and it's hard to tell exactly where you are when you're out there. Is that the new stove?

ARON. It's the latest design, they've only just brought them out. They're going to make them for the army.

FELIX. It's a Krups.

ARON. Methylated spirit.

FELIX *examines the stove.*

A sound piece of German engineering. (*Beat.*) Would you like some coffee when it's ready?

FELIX. Of course and make it strong. Thanks for bringing us here, Eva. I'd never have thought to come this side. I must swim more at night. I'll make it a rule: swim in lakes with friends. I'm going to miss all this so much.

EVA. You must visit us.

FELIX. I will as often as I can.

EVA. You must promise.

EVA continues to dry herself.

FELIX. Let me help you there, Eva.

EVA. Thanks, Felix.

FELIX. Let me do your back.

He begins to dry her.

EVA. And Aron, you must do my back too.

EVA throws him a towel.

FELIX. I'll do your front then.

EVA. That would be lovely but another time.

FELIX. There's nothing nicer than having your front slowly but firmly dried.

EVA. I'll remember that.

FELIX. And if you need any help getting dressed . . .

EVA. Felix!

FELIX (*beat*). How d'you hold on to these moments – these feelings, this life – ?

ARON. I wish I knew.

FELIX. What about you, Eva?

EVA. Me? I assemble a picture. The moon on the water, the buoy, the trees, the smell of pine and stone, the catch of air. I store the details in my head and I make a memory.

ARON. What about the stove. Does the stove get into your picture?

EVA. If it's making hot coffee it certainly does.

Pause.

FELIX. I've been thinking about your grand plan.

ARON. The shoe shop?

FELIX. Yes, how far have you got with it?

ARON. Quite far.

FELIX. Initial plan far or purchase far?

ARON. Initial plan plus three backers far.

FELIX. Why don't we work together?

ARON. In business, you mean?

FELIX. Yes. We could do it together.

ARON. But you're leaving.

FELIX. I don't want to go.

ARON. I don't know.

FELIX. How long have we been friends? Since we were six.
    I don't want to leave. What do you think, Eva?

EVA. A Jew and a Gentile in business?

FELIX. Who cares?

EVA. Everyone will care.

FELIX. Let them.

EVA. We've been friends for so long – it would be wonderful.

FELIX. Good. And you will play the piano at our opening.

EVA. Of course.

ARON. And you will model the women's shoes for us.

EVA. I will model the women's shoes for you.

FELIX. And the men's shoes. You must! If any man sees shoes
    on those beautiful legs of yours they will buy three pairs.

ARON. Wait a minute. I haven't agreed anything yet.

FELIX. I would like it so much, Aron.

EVA. Isn't that what you want? Isn't that what we all want?

ARON. I need to think about it, that's all.

EVA. Oh Aron, you must.

ARON. I'll have to see. (*Beat.*) Let's drink coffee first.

FELIX. There's only one cup.

EVA. We can all share it.

ARON. We'll share everything.

FELIX. Everything?

ARON. Everything.

EVA. Oh Aron, that's wonderful.

ARON. Sshh!

EVA. What's that?

They listen.

FELIX. What did you hear?

ARON. Happiness.

They sit quietly and drink together from the cup.

Scene Four

BEN. Two thousand and six. Bethlehem.

The sound of an armoured car.

BASHAR is cleaning the floor with soap and water. ISAAC enters.

ISAAC (*banging on the door*). I'm back.

BASHAR. I can see that.

ISAAC. They're here.

BASHAR. Yes.

ISAAC. You can hear them?

BASHAR. I hear them.

ISAAC. We are requisitioning this house under Section 148/176/C.

BASHAR. You told me already.

ISAAC. We will be demolishing the part of your house that is less than eighty metres from the security Wall.

BASHAR. I know. We went through it yesterday.

ISAAC *walks to a big bowl of fruit.*

ISAAC. It's fresh.

BASHAR. I got it this morning.

ISAAC. Why did you do that?

BASHAR. I like fruit.

ISAAC (*lifting a bunch of flowers*). And these?

BASHAR. I like flowers, the perfume is fine.

ISAAC. You should have arranged for everything to be taken away.

BASHAR. Everything has been arranged.

ISAAC. The piano is still here.

BASHAR. Everything has been organised.

ISAAC. Play a tune.

BASHAR. No.

ISAAC. You should. You have the plans to the house?

BASHAR. No.

ISAAC. Any architect's drawings?

BASHAR. No. Why?

ISAAC. I want to make sure it's clean.

BASHAR. Clean?

ISAAC. I'm trying to be helpful. My dad was a builder.

BASHAR. Your father builds and you tear it down.

ISAAC. Some of the others would ensure it was not clean. When they take down your wall, they would break the foundations of the house next door. Your neighbours must be worried.

BASHAR. Yes, they are.

ISAAC. Find me drawings and then you can reassure them that their house will still stand. I can do a clean job if you find me the plans.

BASHAR. I don't know where they are.

ISAAC. You must look. Then we can take down your kitchen wall carefully.

BASHAR. My father lived here. All my children were born here. I grew up here. You see the tree outside? My father grew it from a pip, from a fruit he bought at the market. When you have finished there will be nothing outside and your Wall will stretch for hundreds of kilometres.

ISAAC. When it is finished.

BASHAR. You make it of concrete. It has fences and razor wire and motion sensors and watch towers. Within eighty metres of the Wall is a military zone and you make it so high I cannot see the sunset.

ISAAC. It's a security wall.

BASHAR. There is no security. It's just a wall.

ISAAC. You mentioned a tree.

BASHAR. In spring, my children swing on it and in the winter we cover it with decorations. Look, I will show you.

He stops cleaning and they go to the window.

ISAAC. That one?

BASHAR. Yes, that one.

ISAAC. That tree will be gone by tomorrow morning.

Beat.

BASHAR. Will you clear it away?

ISAAC. Yes.

BASHAR. When you knock down my house, you will take away the rubble.

ISAAC. Yes.

BASHAR. I would have liked some of it.

ISAAC. You want the rubble?

BASHAR. My rubble.

ISAAC. It will be taken away.

BASHAR. Everything will be taken away?

ISAAC. All the rubble will go.

BASHAR. Where will you take it?

ISAAC. I don't take it anywhere.

BASHAR. Where does it go?

ISAAC. I don't know.

BASHAR. It must go somewhere.

ISAAC. Look, I'm demolition.

BASHAR. How can you do this?

ISAAC. Look, it's nothing personal.

BASHAR. This is my house. This is my land.

ISAAC. This is our land.

BASHAR. We share the land.

ISAAC. This is the law.

BASHAR. Military Law.

ISAAC *exits.*

BEN. Remember, it's the end for him.

HUW. Do I just stand here, then?

BEN. Yes, you do. He's losing everything as we watch him.

BASHAR, *standing, stares out into the future.*

Silence. He shakes.

Back to the rehearsal room.

OLLY. Ben.

BEN (*playing*). Ssh!

OLLY (*as* BEN *finishes*). Can I speak?

BEN. If it's about the rewrites, no.

OLLY. It's the meter. I really can't have it towed away. I just keep thinking about it.

BEN. Hurry.

OLLY *exits.*

LEE. Anybody for tea?

BARBARA. Not for me, thanks. I've just had imaginary coffee.

She shudders.

SIMON. Nor me.

DAN. It wasn't that bad.

HUW. I'll make the tea. One of the best things I learnt as a young actor – make a list of tea requests and cover it in cellophane. No spoiling when things get spilt!

LEE. Why don't we get a toaster?

HUW. What's that?

LEE. We should all chip in and get a toaster. They're not very expensive.

HUW. Maybe I'll make Café Arabi.

SIMON. Tea and toast. Perfect!

DAN. I'm in.

BARBARA. Me too.

LEE. I can't see the point.

SIMON. Well, you wouldn't. Just because you can't cook apples and yogurt in a toaster doesn't mean . . .

BEN. I can't see the point either.

HUW. Nor me.

LEE. Casting vote to Olly, then.

BEN. Where is he? Doesn't take that long to feed a meter.

SIMON. Oh, he'll want a toaster. He drives one.

BARBARA. Don't let him hear you say that.

BEN. We won't wait. Simon, Barbara, Memory Five.

Scene Five

BEN. Eva's memory of Aron. Nineteen thirty-four.

BEN *plays the Bach on the piano quietly in the background.*

EVA. Our music.

ARON. German music.

EVA. I brought you back a present.

ARON. You look so sexy; like a mermaid.

EVA. A present. For you to give to me.

ARON. For me to give to you?

EVA. That's right. I got it whilst I was away.

ARON. You look delicious.

EVA. Just open it.

ARON *opens the box to find the engagement ring.*

ARON. It's a ring.

EVA. Now give it to me.

ARON. I haven't touched you yet.

EVA. Marry me.

ARON. Yes.

EVA. Touch me.

ARON. Your smell.

> BEN *plays.*

> Dance with me.

> ARON *and* EVA *dance.*

> We'll have a garden. I'll grow sunflowers. And tulips and marigolds. And thousands of dandelions.

EVA. And children?

ARON. Yes, and thousands of children.

EVA. You would like children?

ARON. Yes, I would. (*He takes out another jewellery box.*) Will you have this?

> *She opens the box.*

EVA. Two rings?

ARON. Why not?

> *She puts the ring on.*

EVA. Aron.

ARON. Kiss my neck?

EVA. I have something to say.

ARON. Just kiss my neck?

EVA. I have something to ask you.

ARON. Kiss me.

EVA. I need you to look after two boys. They're my cousin's sons, just for a couple of months.

ARON. How old are they?

EVA. Three and five.

ARON. Two boys?

EVA. They're my cousin's, they're in trouble.

ARON. Just a couple of months?

EVA. Just 'til things blow over.

ARON. Are they good?

EVA. They're boys. They're three and five.

ARON. Of course, of course, if you kiss me now.

EVA. I need you to listen to me.

ARON. I'm listening.

EVA. Aron, I'm pregnant.

ARON. Eva!

EVA. Just one.

ARON. Well, it's a start.

EVA. I'm home.

The music finishes.

Scene Six

1990. EVA *and* PETER *in the flat.* PETER *is banging on the door.*

PETER. Open the door. (*He starts knocking again loudly.*) Let me in.

EVA. Go away.

PETER *bangs on the door.*

I'm asleep.

PETER *carries on banging.*

PETER. I'm hurt.

PETER *bangs furiously.*

My leg.

EVA. Get out! Leave me alone!

PETER. It's hurting.

EVA. Please.

PETER. I'm not going.

EVA. You smell. (EVA *removes an empty half-bottle of vodka from his pocket.*) Did you drink all this?

PETER. I think so.

EVA. All of it?

PETER. I said.

EVA. You must wash yourself. Do you have clean clothes? Where are your bags?

PETER. I lost everything.

EVA. You've nothing?

PETER. I've been sick.

EVA. Here.

She hands PETER *a T-shirt.*

PETER. Thank you.

EVA. I don't want you here.

PETER. I've lost everything.

EVA. You must go. You will go tomorrow.

PETER. It's too big.

EVA. You're too small.

PETER. I was chased.

EVA. Chased? Where were you chased?

PETER. Along Reichstagplatz.

EVA. Who by?

PETER. By two men and a dog.

EVA. What sort of dog?

PETER. An Alsatian.

EVA. An Alsatian chased you?

PETER. It was a large dog. It bit my leg. It wouldn't let go. I screamed. The guard was laughing.

EVA. The guard?

PETER. The guard.

EVA. Why did the dog do that?

PETER. I don't know. I only bent down to stroke it.

EVA. You bent down to stroke a guard dog?

PETER. It dragged me by the leg. I was drunk. Don't worry, I'm sober now . . . more or less.

EVA. Drunk in the Reichstag?

PETER. I just climbed over some wire fencing. I had to be drunk to go there. All those Nazi ghosts in there. The Reichstag should have been flattened years ago.

EVA. It's a building.

PETER. It's a symbol of hatred. How can you live here? In Berlin, in Germany? How can you stay here? I told that to the guard with the dog. I said, your city is beautiful and it's still *judenrein*.

EVA. You said that?

PETER. The man pushed me over. He kicked me.

EVA. You were drunk.

PETER. They say the Reichstag will be rebuilt. Civil servants will walk along the same corridors that Hitler used.

EVA. Hitler did not walk those corridors. Hitler burnt down the Reichstag. You are inaccurate.

PETER. I'm inaccurate. What a crime! So where did he work? On the moon?

EVA. Why do you do this?

PETER. Hitler was in Berlin, his bunker's close by.

EVA. Hitler this, Hitler that. It's past, past.

PETER. You just don't listen, do you?

EVA. You are a parasite, a thing crabbing around. These memories I have, they are not yours.

PETER. They belong to me, too.

EVA. No, no, they belong only to me, and to all who died.

Beat.

PETER. You only pretend you've coped.

EVA. I have functioned.

PETER. You hide, your life is tiny. You were well off, now you're poor. You were a pianist, so what did you do? You washed dishes. No wonder I got drunk when I left you. I bought a bottle of vodka, never done it before, warms you up if you drink it fast enough.

EVA. You are one of those worms that suck blood. My blood.

PETER. I want to know everything. It is my right.

EVA. Your father never comes and when you come you get drunk.

PETER. Your son will never come. He wouldn't be able to stand it. All those friends gone. The rest of his family disappeared. He won't be back. You know that. (*Beat.*) Let me take you out.

EVA. Take me out? Now?

PETER. I want to take you somewhere.

EVA. It's late.

PETER. Please let me take you out.

EVA. You don't want to take me out.

PETER. Let me take you to a cafe.

EVA. No.

PETER. A restaurant then, somewhere where we can get something good to eat.

EVA. No.

PETER. Let's get out of here.

EVA. You could take me to a circus.

PETER. A circus!

EVA. I want to go to a circus.

PETER. A circus it is.

EVA. Maybe I will drink a glass of champagne and we will laugh and I will wet the streets with my spit. Perhaps we will dance.

PETER. Hold me?

EVA. You play.

> BEN *plays twelve bars of the Goldberg Variations.*

> The pulse was unsteady.

PETER. I reached bar twelve; it's something.

EVA. Bar twelve.

PETER. Yes.

EVA. Bach is a genius. How you can do this to him I do not know.

PETER. You're not normal, are you?

EVA. That's right, insult me.

PETER. It's not an insult. Maybe I've inherited something, maybe it's genetic.

EVA. Blame me, why don't you? They're your problems, not mine. Hold me.

> PETER *walks over to her and is about to touch her.*

> Hold me.

> *They hold each other.*

Back to the rehearsal room. OLLY *re-enters.*

BARBARA. Did you get it sorted?

OLLY. Yeah, for half an hour. Thanks

BEN. Why only half an hour?

OLLY. It's all the meter would let me have.

SIMON. Olly, what do you think about a toaster?

BEN. Not now! On.

BARBARA (*to* OLLY). What took you so long?

OLLY. Negotiations with the parking meter.

Scene Seven

FELIX. The architect's only just finished them.

ARON. The atrium includes more than one storey?

FELIX. That's what atriums are!

ARON. You can't put shoes in an atrium.

FELIX. We've been through this a hundred times.

ARON. We agreed not to build a large section without a floor.

FELIX. Sometimes I wonder about your general education. The atrium is important to the dignity of the space.

ARON. So you build with nowhere to go?

FELIX. An atrium gives a feeling of light and space, people feel better, as people look up they see beauty. Our shoe shop will be the most glamorous in Berlin.

ARON. It's a shoe shop.

FELIX. It will be light. People love light, it cheers them.

ARON. Shoes. We're selling shoes. People will be looking at their feet.

FELIX. Your problem is that you don't shop, you just buy things. Now look at these plans with me again.

ARON. Let me see them.

They study the plans.

FELIX. So people enter here, where it's quite small and rather normal and then they walk through into here and suddenly they are in a brightly lit space with the light streaming onto their faces.

Pause.

ARON. Build it.

FELIX. What?

ARON. You're right. People need light.

FELIX. I'm amazed.

ARON. It's a good idea. It's a prime location.

FELIX. You mean it?

ARON. I said.

FELIX. After all these months you've changed your mind?

ARON. Absolutely.

EVA *enters.*

FELIX. Eva! He's said yes to the atrium!

EVA. You persuaded him. How exciting!

ARON. I'm just slower than you two, that's all.

EVA. Which is why we're three.

ARON. I'll go and check on the boys.

ARON *exits.*

FELIX (*taking flowers from piano*). I picked these. They're for you.

EVA. The perfume is intoxicating.

FELIX. A kiss.

He kisses EVA. *She withdraws.*

EVA. Felix.

FELIX. You look beautiful, Eva.

EVA. Felix . . .

FELIX. You do. You look stunning.

EVA. Thank you.

FELIX. My compliments are too much.

EVA. No . . . No, I love compliments.

FELIX. You do?

EVA. The flowers are beautiful.

Pause.

FELIX. I dream that one day you'll come running to me.

EVA. I'm very fond of you, Felix.

FELIX. I missed you whilst you were away. I thought of you all the time.

EVA. My classes were well received.

FELIX. So why did you return?

EVA. Love makes you do irrational things.

FELIX. Love.

EVA. Yes. Love. (*Beat.*) I'm engaged.

FELIX. Engaged?

EVA. Engaged to be married.

FELIX. You met someone?

EVA. Yes.

FELIX. I'm delighted for you, whoever he is, he's a very lucky man.

ARON *enters.*

ARON. It's me.

FELIX. You.

ARON. Me.

Pause.

FELIX. I'm so pleased. I didn't know . . . I really am delighted
for you both, my two dear friends, how . . . extraordinary . . .
that I did not realise . . . congratulations!

EVA *shows him her hand.*

You have two rings.

EVA *points to her womb.*

EVA. There's going to be a baby.

FELIX. I have to go! I'm delighted for you both . . . for all
three of you.

FELIX *exits.*

ARON. He'll get over it.

ARON *picks up the plans.*

EVA. I had no idea he would be so upset.

ARON. It'll sort itself out; these things do.

EVA. I hope so. How were the boys?

ARON. Terrible. The little one pissed all over the kitchen floor.
It was some sort of protest, I suppose.

EVA. Their mother wrote to me asking if they could stay
longer.

ARON. Of course they can. They're lovely boys. I told you
I wanted thousands. They're welcome to stay.

Scene Eight

BEN. Two thousand and six. Bethlehem. The noise of the bulldozer.

ISAAC. Old man, you must come with me.

BASHAR. I will not come.

ISAAC. You are like my uncle. Next you will tell me that I should get my hair cut.

BASHAR. Perhaps you should.

ISAAC. I like you. I'm not meant to.

BASHAR. We're not so different. It is a war between people with small differences.

ISAAC. I will radio for help.

BASHAR. I have decided to stay.

ISAAC. You are stupid. My uncle is stupid too.

BASHAR. Would you like some tea?

ISAAC. Thank you.

BASHAR. It's better with sugar?

ISAAC. They will make you move.

BASHAR. Lemon?

ISAAC. You were born in this house?

BASHAR. And my father and his father.

ISAAC. You lived in this house?

BASHAR. All of us. Yes.

ISAAC. You will be buried in this house.

BASHAR. It is a crime.

ISAAC. I like this tea.

BASHAR. Why do you do this?

ISAAC. Why didn't you fight the eviction order?

BASHAR. To fight the eviction order I have to go from here to Jerusalem – to the offices of the military to register the complaint. And this is the other side of the Wall. To get to it I must pass through the checkpoint and you will not let me through it.

ISAAC. The checkpoints are nothing to do with me.

BASHAR. More tea?

ISAAC. Thanks.

BASHAR. You cannot push us all into the sea.

ISAAC. Please come.

BASHAR. The Wall will lock you in.

ISAAC. And keep you out.

BASHAR. Why aren't you in the Lebanon?

ISAAC. Eyesight. My eyesight's bad.

BASHAR. Yes. I remember the maps.

ISAAC. This Wall will help you.

BASHAR. No, it won't. Might buy a few votes, I suppose.

ISAAC. For Hamas probably.

BASHAR. I didn't vote.

ISAAC. Nor did I, but lots did. More than in the West, anyway.

BASHAR (*chuckling*). Oh yes – the West! If you can't vote, you want to. If you can vote, you can't be bothered. They call it democracy.

ISAAC. I've got to go now. Please come with me.

BASHAR. Why do you care?

ISAAC. I don't, but you're like my uncle. He's stupid too.

BASHAR. You said.

ISAAC. Thanks for the tea.

BASHAR. Were you born in Israel?

ISAAC. Of course.

BASHAR. And your father?

ISAAC. Odessa.

BASHAR. And your mother?

ISAAC. Frankfurt.

BASHAR. Why did they come here?

ISAAC. Don't know. Didn't belong, I suppose.

BASHAR. You don't belong anywhere, do you?

ISAAC. Nor do you.

BASHAR. So why do we do this to each other?

ISAAC. I don't know. I don't know. I've told you, I don't know! I'm just carrying out orders.

BASHAR. I'll wash the cups.

Noise of the bulldozer.

Interval.

Scene Nine

BEN. Okay. Nineteen thirty-seven. The allotment. Summer. The picnic.

EVA is dressed up and laying out the picnic. Birds are singing. She places a rug on the ground. ARON enters, also dressed well, and kisses her lightly.

ARON. Big day.

EVA. An amazing, eventful day.

ARON. He'll be in a rush. I haven't got long, he'll say, I've got business to sort out.

EVA. Maybe it's a good thing.

ARON. There's no choice.

EVA. It's wrong.

ARON. The sun shines.

EVA. It's getting hotter.

ARON. I like the heat.

They both stare at the sun, it's healing.

EVA. I'm fine.

ARON. I'm all right.

EVA and ARON kiss. FELIX enters. He carries a small case.

FELIX. What's this?

EVA. It's a picnic; we wanted to make this civilised.

FELIX. Why do you kiss in front of me?

EVA. Sorry.

FELIX. I'm in a rush.

EVA. The sun shines. Coffee will be here soon.

ARON. Coffee?

EVA. A quick cup.

FELIX. All right. A quick cup.

> ARON *goes and gets the stove.* EVA *and* FELIX *sit on the rug, staring at the sun.*

EVA. The sun's hot today.

FELIX. Yes, it is.

EVA. It lifts my spirits.

FELIX. Does it?

EVA. Look at the swallows, they're so busy.

FELIX. Swallows are my favourite birds.

EVA. Mine too.

> *They watch the swallows.*

FELIX. I look for you everywhere: on streets, in trains, in shops. I look for you in cafes, in restaurants, in libraries, through windows, down alleys, in the evening, during the day . . . Walk with me now.

EVA. Don't be ridiculous.

FELIX. Walk with me.

EVA. No.

> *They wait together.*

FELIX. Things are going to get worse.

EVA. How do you know?

FELIX. Walk to safety with me. Now.

EVA. Safety?

FELIX. Just stand. And walk away with me. Then you'll be safe.

> *Pause.*

EVA. No.

FELIX. You can bring the children.

Pause.

EVA. No.

FELIX. For their sakes. As well as yours.

EVA. I can't.

FELIX. I can look after you all.

EVA. The children?

FELIX. Yes.

EVA. All three of them?

FELIX. Yes.

EVA. My cousin's sons Joshua and Elie, and my own little Dov?

FELIX. Yes. Joshua, Elie and Dov.

She begins to stand, then sits down again.

ARON *returns with coffee.*

ARON. Let's get it over with, shall we?

FELIX *takes out the papers and gives a pen to* ARON.

FELIX. I've marked out the contracts. You must sign five times.

ARON. The shop has done so well and so quickly. The atrium was a good idea.

FELIX. It's not the atrium that was good for business. It's National Socialism. I'm giving you a good price. With the money you can do anything you like. Anyway, it's not personal; you're not allowed to own it anymore. It's the law.

EVA. It has to be done.

ARON. I feel sick.

EVA. We'll be fine.

FELIX. Sorry about this but can we speed up? I have to go to a meeting in a minute. (*He pulls a swastika armband out of his bag and puts it on.*) There's no need to look like that. I'm going to a meeting, that's all. We have to wear them. You know what this lot's like with their badges.

When this has all blown over we'll sort things out. It's been so busy lately.

EVA. You aren't telling us something. What are you trying to say?

FELIX. Hitler came into our shop. My shop. Why shouldn't he – we're the best shoe shop and we're the closest to the Chancellery. His entourage crowded it out and he chose two pairs of slippers and I noticed the redness of his hair. I wrapped them up carefully and as I handed them to one of his staff a most surprising sensation came over me: gratitude.

Scene Ten

BASHAR. Have you come to kill me?

ISAAC. No. But I want to.

BASHAR. Why?

ISAAC. Last night you blew up a bus – men, women, children, fourteen dead more than fifty injured.

BASHAR. Last night your airforce bombed a school, thirty children, three teachers.

The next two lines are spoken together.

ISAAC. Everywhere – bits of body, arms, legs, teeth – I saw a foot, a foot!

BASHAR. Heads, half heads, bits of flesh, blood and stink. The stink!

ISAAC. Yours was deliberate. Ours was an accident.

BASHAR. Accident?! You drop leaflets and you threaten, you broadcast and you call it an accident?!

ISAAC. You sacrifice your own and call them heroes and martyrs and plaster the walls with their pictures . . .

BASHAR. And you trap us behind these walls with nothing to do and nowhere to go. No wonder we blow up. You make ghettoes. Where did you learn that?

ISAAC. Last night a rocket hit my street. Now I don't have an upstairs either.

BASHAR. Your tanks have made thousands homeless, totally homeless and you talk of upstairs!

ISAAC. You celebrate. We apologise.

BASHAR. You didn't apologise when you blew up King David's Hotel in forty-seven.

ISAAC. We had to have somewhere to live.

BASHAR. Lebensraum.

ISAAC. What?

BASHAR. We need somewhere to live too!

ISAAC. Then go to Jordan, to Syria, to Lebanon, to . . . .

BASHAR. They won't let us in!

ISAAC. So why blame us?

BASHAR. We're the Jews of the Middle East. No one wants us.

ISAAC. Then go back to being nomads.

BASHAR. You stole our land. All the terraces and stones and olive groves taken from my fathers and their fathers and their fathers; generations.

ISAAC. We did not steal it, you sold most of it to us. You liked us when we first came. All that money.

BASHAR. I see foreigners on Arab land. Hassidim Jews with their sickly skin and their black hats and ringlets. Young Israelis with their arrogance and ruthlessness.

ISAAC. And I see corrupt governments, corrupt families, jails full of dissidents, women repressed and children sacrificed. Tell me one Arab democracy.

BASHAR. We don't want democracy. We want peace.

ISAAC. We offered you peace. Over and over again. But you don't want peace. You want us gone. But we will fight. One holocaust is enough.

BASHAR. You're everywhere and you are not wanted anywhere.

ISAAC. Do you really believe seventy-two virgins will be there for them when they die?

BASHAR. What?

ISAAC. Doesn't say their ages, does it?

BASHAR. Their ages?

ISAAC. You know how old those virgins are?

BASHAR. What are you talking about?

ISAAC. You blow yourself up, you go straight to heaven, you walk into a room lined with silk, you have an erection like a broom handle and there they are – seventy-two eighty-five-year-old virgins, with no teeth, staring at you.

BASHAR. My children will not be bombers – but your children will be soldiers.

ISAAC. You are being used, can't you see that? By Iran, by Syria – new weapons, new money. Is that what you want to be? The new Hizbollah?

BASHAR. Excuses. You always find excuses. A hostage, Iran, Hizbollah, Hamas. Any excuse to beat us. We are now the only people you *can* beat.

ISAAC. We were trying to save civilians.

BASHAR. And you failed.

ISAAC. But we care. You burn, torture, maim in the name of Islam and when any of you get money, you buy weapons.

BASHAR. You kill our children.

ISAAC. You kill your own children.

BASHAR. Wherever you go, death follows.

ISAAC. We make the desert bloom!

BASHAR. And we who have lived here for generations are its fruit.

Scene Eleven

BEN. Eva and Peter. Nineteen ninety.

> PETER *enters. He holds a bottle of champagne and pours out two glasses.*

> EVA *holds the drink.*

EVA. To the circus.

PETER. The circus!

EVA. I've never seen a chicken do that.

PETER. It was amazing.

EVA. A pony trots around the ring. A dog rides on the back of the pony and the chicken rides the dog.

PETER. The chicken is on them both.

EVA. Can you believe they call this a circus?

PETER. It was more like a farmyard.

EVA. It was. I have never seen such talent in a chicken. In its little scarf and its little hat! Unbelievable.

PETER. You liked the weightlifter?

EVA. I did; he was strong.

PETER. Meaning?

EVA. I can tell you one thing: if it all goes wrong you could always join it. Perhaps you could play the first few bars of the Bach with a chicken on your head.

PETER. And the synagogue? What was it like to see that again?

EVA. It interested me.

PETER. You remembered where it was.

EVA. Of course.

PETER. Now the Wall is down you can visit it.

EVA. It's been a long time.

PETER. You didn't spit.

EVA. I spat. Yes, I spat.

PETER. You did?

EVA. I spat in many places.

PETER. I didn't notice.

EVA. I spit discreetly.

PETER. Why haven't you done this before?

EVA. Don't.

PETER. You enjoyed it so much. (*Beat.*) I want to know about my father.

EVA. Not now.

PETER. Tell me.

EVA. Will you just stop it! Can you not for a moment stop thinking about all this history? History has gone. History is not here. Why can't you be more like Joshua?

PETER. Joshua? I thought you didn't hear from him.

EVA. Joshua, Elie, I get confused.

PETER. Have you told him you're ill?

EVA. He won't want to know.

PETER. You must let him know. You must tell him. I want you to. You must write.

EVA. I don't feel like it.

PETER. Write. Come on.

EVA. There's no paper.

PETER. There's paper here. I want you to write to him.

EVA. I don't want to.

PETER. You must. I insist. For once, I absolutely insist.

EVA. Why should I?

PETER. I won't meet him, will I?

EVA. No. You won't.

PETER. I want you to write, please dictate. I'll use your typewriter.

EVA. Please don't.

PETER. Why not?

EVA. I lay on those boys. I protected them with my body.

PETER. You write it then.

He gives her paper.

EVA *writes.*

My dear Elie. Come quickly. I am not well. Eva.

It's short.

EVA. So?

PETER. He'll be devastated, surely you must understand that.

EVA. Don't go on.

PETER. It needs to be longer.

EVA (*reading as she writes*). P.S. I hope the family is well.

PETER. It's too short.

EVA. I cannot hide it from him.

PETER. You're dying.

EVA. Much worse things have happened. You write it.

PETER. That would be stupid.

EVA. I don't care what you say.

PETER (*reading as he writes*). 'Dear Elie, I am ill. It is true that I do not have long to live. Perhaps you could contact me as soon as you can, Eva. Now sign it.'

EVA. Why should I?

PETER. Just do it.

She signs it.

The address?

EVA. I will do it later.

PETER. Let me write the address.

EVA. I don't have it.

PETER. It will be on his letters. Let me see.

EVA. No. Peter. Please. Not now. All right. You understand. Not yet. I am not ready for it yet.

Scene Twelve

BEN. Nineteen forty-two. The allotment. Night. Winter.

ARON *enters, wearing his yellow star. Someone approaches.* FELIX *enters, wearing his uniform.*

FELIX. It had to be you.

ARON. It's been a while.

FELIX. A neighbour of yours wrote to us. Some are living on their allotments; then I realised. How long have you been here?

ARON. Six or seven weeks.

FELIX. Not long then.

ARON. Are you going to arrest me?

FELIX. Orders.

ARON. What can we give you? There's nothing more I can give you. I gave you the shop.

FELIX. I bought the shop from you. (*He picks up the stove.*) Still going?

ARON. Yes. You can have it if you let me go. I've nothing else to give you.

FELIX. I can have it anyway. Where will you go?

ARON. There's nowhere.

FELIX. The city is full of informers. There are Jews who report other Jews to us. It's quite funny.

ARON. Do you have a razor? If I could get clean. If I could borrow some clothes, a suit perhaps . . . you could bring me these?

FELIX. No.

ARON. Could you get me a uniform?

FELIX. You're a Jew.

ARON. But I don't really look different, do I? Do I? I'm German.

FELIX. You should have left. You had the money.

ARON. No one would take us.

FELIX. No one at all? How can that be true?

ARON. No country will give any of us visas.

FELIX. What about Britain?

ARON. No.

FELIX. America?

ARON. No.

FELIX. Australia? South Africa? New Zealand?

ARON. No country will take us. Not one.

FELIX. Are you hungry?

ARON. No.

FELIX. Here.

> FELIX *gives* ARON *food.*

ARON. Thank you. I'll save it.

> *He eats it ravenously.*

FELIX. You can have this, too.

> ARON *saves it.*

ARON. When summer comes, this will have so much life in it. Look after it.

FELIX. I will.

ARON. We made love here. I conceived my son here.

FELIX. Where are the others?

ARON. I don't know.

FELIX. Where's Eva? Where are the boys?

> ARON *offers him the stove.*

ARON. Take it.

FELIX. I don't want it.

ARON. It's the memories you don't want.

FELIX. They're hiding in the shed, aren't they?

> FELIX *goes into the shed. He drags* EVA *out. She also wears a yellow star.*

There's only two in there. Where's the other one?

ARON. In England.

FELIX. How?

ARON. He went on the kindertransport.

FELIX. The mercy trains full of little children. You must hope we don't cross the channel. But why only one?

ARON. There was only enough money for one.

FELIX. So you chose your own child?

EVA. Yes, I chose. All families had to choose.

FELIX. When did you do this?

EVA. Two years ago.

FELIX. Tell me what happened.

EVA. Do I have to?

FELIX. I want to hear what happened.

EVA. The train went from here to the Hook of Holland and then to Harwich. I persuaded myself he was going on holiday and that he would be back soon. It's what I told him. Before he left I bathed him. He was five and so his body was like cream. I washed his hair, he complained, but it was for me, not for him and I scratched his scalp and cascaded warm water over him, I knew it was the last time. I held him tight and the hot perfume of his skin entered my nostrils. I dressed him and we picked up his bags and I carried one and he the other. We caught a tram and I took him to the barrier at the Grünewaldstrasse where all the other children were. There his hand slipped mine. It surprised me, the speed. I tried to keep my eyes on him but he was whisked away. The officials took him. I waved the train goodbye. It was laden with children. Some of them smiled and waved. After it left, there were hundreds of parents left on the platform. We were so quiet. We were Jews and we didn't want any attention on ourselves. I walked home. It took me hours. When I returned to the flat, the water was still in the bath. It had gone cold but I couldn't let it out. I lay on his bed and I covered myself with his clothes.

Beat.

What can we give you to let us go?

FELIX. There's nothing you can give me.

ARON. We only have the stove and he doesn't want that.

FELIX. Your neighbours have reported you. I'll have to take you.

 EVA *takes off her coat and unbuttons her dress.*

ARON. No.

FELIX. Stop it.

EVA. It's what you want.

ARON. Please, Eva, not this.

FELIX. It's not what I want.

EVA. Take me, Felix.

FELIX. I don't want to.

EVA. Take me. Any way you like.

FELIX. No.

EVA. Take me. Then let me go. Take me and let us all go. In the shed. Now. Let yourself. Look at you. I know you want to and now you can. You can have me. Finally. I'm all yours. To the victor the spoils.

FELIX. Will you forgive me?

EVA. We'll forgive you if you let us go.

 EVA *and* FELIX *go into the shed.*

 ARON *waits.*

 EVA *and* FELIX *emerge out of the shed.*

FELIX. Aron, you must stay here. The two boys and Eva will come with me. You should wait until just before dawn and then come to Allasee.

ARON. Then what will happen?

FELIX. I'll meet you there. (*He writes a note and gives it to* ARON.) If anyone stops you, show them this.

ARON. Will they be safe?

FELIX. They'll all be safe with me now.

ARON. You're sure?

FELIX. Yes, they'll be safe.

ARON *touches* EVA*'s face.*

FELIX *and* EVA *exit.* ARON *goes to the shed. Returns with a rope. Stands.*

Scene Thirteen

ISAAC. It's time to go.

BASHAR. Yes.

ISAAC. I'm sorry about . . .

BASHAR. So am I.

ISAAC. I didn't mean . . .

BASHAR. No, nor did I.

ISAAC. Sorry.

Beat.

BASHAR. Could I have a last look?

ISAAC. Yes.

BASHAR *looks around.*

BASHAR. I don't suppose we'll meet again.

ISAAC. No.

BASHAR. Our children perhaps.

ISAAC. Perhaps. (*Beat.*) Any idea what yours will do?

BASHAR. We're hoping Leila and Safi will become doctors or lawyers. I'd settle for accountants. Abdel's the artistic one. They'll probably end up running corner shops and driving taxis.

As they go:

ISAAC. I want mine to go to America.

BASHAR. Somewhere where there aren't any walls.

ISAAC. Yes. Where there aren't any walls.

Scene Fourteen.

BEN. Nineteen ninety. Eva's flat.

PETER. My grandfather haunts me.

EVA. You're like him.

PETER. Am I?

EVA. When I first saw you at the door. For a moment I thought you were him.

PETER. Something terrible happened, I know.

EVA. I will tell you if you promise me one thing.

PETER. What?

EVA. You will leave.

PETER. I promise.

EVA. He killed himself.

PETER. How?

EVA. He hanged himself.

PETER. Where did he do it?

EVA. On his allotment.

> ARON *stands in the doorway.*

PETER. Why the allotment?

EVA. He was hiding. Quite a lot of us hid there. It was common but neighbours reported us.

> *Beat.*

PETER. There's something else.

EVA. No. That's it.

PETER. There's more, I know. I won't leave until you tell me everything.

EVA. It's over.

PETER. Oh, come on.

EVA. It was my fault.

PETER. Why?

EVA. I let another man have me. I thought I was helping. (*To* ARON.) Forgive me. (*To* PETER.) Every day I think about it.

PETER. So why didn't he let you all go?

EVA. I don't know. But he didn't. If only I had done something different. Hold my hand.

PETER *walks to her and offers his hand.*

I survived.

PETER. Can you tell me?

EVA. Tell you what?

PETER. Just tell me.

EVA. After Kristallnacht, we sold our business to Felix and we raised fifty pounds.

PETER. Why fifty pounds?

EVA. The English government would only accept a child if we could provide fifty pounds. It was a lot of money, enough for a house. Fifty pounds for a life. To value a life; it is so stupid.

BARBARA (*out of character*). What does it change?

BARBARA *begins to walk out of the rehearsal room.*

BEN. Barbara.

BARBARA. I'm going out for a breath of fresh air.

BEN. We'll take five minutes.

BEN *and* BARBARA *exit.*

OLLY *switches the kettle on. The water bubbles. He arranges the cups.*

OLLY. Do you think I could get to the meter before she comes back?

DAN. He'll be outside, won't he?

OLLY. Yeah, but she looked pretty upset. It can take a while for her to calm down.

DAN. Last time she did it she came back pretty quickly.

BEN *returns.*

LEE. She all right?

BEN. She'll be here in a minute.

OLLY. Do you think she'll get over it? (*Beat.*) My bloody car's probably been towed away by now.

LEE. Is Barbara coming back immediately or can we get a breath of fresh air too?

BEN. She's on her way.

BARBARA *enters.*

BARBARA. Everyone's staring at me.

OLLY. That's because you just walked out.

BARBARA. And since when was that against the law?

OLLY. It's all right for you. He won't let me out. Will you Ben?

BEN. Olly . . .

SIMON. Are you all right?

BARBARA. I'm okay, thanks.

SIMON. Early days.

BARBARA. Just gets to me.

OLLY. You didn't walk past a metallic blue Porsche, did you?

BARBARA. Metallic blue?

OLLY. Yes.

BARBARA. Yeah, I did.

OLLY. You did?

BARBARA. It had loads of stickers on it.

OLLY. Bloody hell.

BARBARA. And one of those yellow clamps on the front wheel.

OLLY. Ben, my car needs me.

He starts to walk out.

BARBARA. Only joking.

OLLY. Thanks!

BEN. Let's carry on. From the end of the last speech please.

BARBARA. From 'When I returned to the flat?'

BEN. Yes, that's fine.

EVA. When I returned to the flat, the water was still in the bath. It had gone cold but I couldn't let it out. I lay on his bed and I covered myself with his clothes.

PETER. Thank you.

EVA. And he survived. I have had much to be thankful for.

PETER. I suppose you do. I often play at this time of night.

BEN *plays the piano.*

EVA. That's good. You're improvising. Good.

He carries on playing.

That's quite good.

PETER. Thank you.

With difficulty, EVA *stands and begins to dance slowly to the music.*

You're dancing.

EVA. So it seems.

PETER. Did my grandfather dance?

EVA. Yes, he did.

PETER. Tell me I'm like him.

EVA. You are. You have come home.

She dances formally and slowly while BEN *plays.*

FELIX *enters holding* ARON, *who has hung himself, in his arms. The rope is still around his neck. They sit down in the room.*

No! No! Not again! Not that memory again. I will not remember that!

PETER *lights a Menorah.*

I hate that thing.

PETER. It's beautiful.

EVA. Why light it now? It's not Chanukkah.

PETER. I want to.

EVA. You're sending God messages for me.

PETER. I'm not.

EVA. You're trying to save my soul. Well, it's too late. I haven't troubled God up until now and I don't intend to start.

PETER. It's pretty.

EVA. I don't think he'll be interested. Read me a letter.

PETER. What?

EVA. They're in the drawer. If you haven't already read them all.

PETER. Of course I haven't.

EVA. They're in the bottom drawer.

PETER *goes to the drawer.*

Choose one at random.

He chooses.

What's the date?

PETER. January twentieth, nineteen sixty-three.

EVA. Read it.

PETER. Eva, it's so green here. Our children play. We have a
kitten – it is tortoise shell. I think of the terrible day all
those years ago. I can hear your screams. You allowed me
this life. Your body over mine. I hold my child in my arms
and am forever grateful.

EVA. What is it?

PETER. The typing.

EVA. I know. I lay on those boys. (*Beat.*) And now we must
dance.

PETER. Dance?

EVA. Yes, come. (*Beat.*) You are awkward.

PETER. Am I?

They dance.

EVA. You are treading on me.

PETER. It's just one of those things; I don't know exactly
where my hands or feet are.

EVA. You don't know where your hands end?

PETER. Not precisely.

EVA. But not knowing where your hands are? Does this mean
that they can wander off on their own?

PETER. It's a condition. It's fairly common. It's called
dyspraxia.

EVA. This could be very useful for people who steal things
from shops. 'But my Lord Judge, I state my case for the
accused: he suffers from asphyxia.'

PETER. Stop it.

EVA. The expensive string of pearls was placed in the accused's pocket by his asphyxiated hands.

PETER. Dyspraxic.

EVA. Fantastic. Your generation. I blame it on you the mess we're in.

A knock at the door.

Who's that?

ISAAC *and* BASHAR *stand up.* ISAAC *stamps his feet.*

ISAAC. It's me. I'm here.

EVA. Go away.

ISAAC. Let me in.

EVA. Go away. I want to sleep.

BASHAR. You must go.

ISAAC. I have to come in.

EVA. Get out. My flat. Get me out! Leave me alone! I need to get up tomorrow. I have so much to do.

ISAAC. It has to be done. The law is a funny thing at the moment.

BASHAR. My kitchen.

EVA. I am an old, dying woman.

ISAAC. You must get out.

BASHAR. I want it to be clean.

PETER. You miss your boys. You saved them.

EVA. I did.

PETER. Only Elie writes.

FELIX. You'll be fine. You'll all be safe with me now.

EVA. Yes.

PETER. Not Josh.

EVA. You talk and talk.

ARON. The atrium.

FELIX. It will be light. Build it.

PETER. You lay on top of them.

EVA. You heard what I said.

PETER. You screamed and lay on their bodies.

EVA. Don't go on!

PETER. The scream of an animal.

EVA. The scream that is inside me that I didn't know I had.
    The Gods froze.

ISAAC. I want it to be clean.

BASHAR. Clean? Yes.

EVA. It's a disgrace.

BASHAR. You're lying.

EVA. What?

BASHAR. It's a lie.

ARON. It's a lie.

EVA. What are you talking about? It is the truth.

    PETER *picks out the letters.*

PETER. You wrote these.

EVA. I want to look outside. Help me! Now! Move! Let me
    see! Outside!

    PETER *helps her to the window. The sun is shining on the
    streets.*

PETER. Tell me.

EVA. I have told you.

PETER. It's not true.

EVA. I'll tell you nothing.

PETER. You write the letters to yourself, don't you?

EVA. So what if I do?

PETER. The boys. It's different to what you said. Tell me. What happened?

EVA. I will not.

PETER. Don't take all these stories to your grave.

EVA. Felix reported us straightaway. We were escorted to the holding place at the Grünewalde railway track where you go before they transport you.

PETER. Carry on.

EVA. The two boys in green hats were with me, squeezing my hands. One of them was crying. 'You boy stop crying' says one of the guards . . . (*As* BARBARA.) I can't go on.

PETER. You must. You must.

BARBARA. No, I won't.

BEN. Why not?

BARBARA. I don't know this speech. I can't do it. I'll have to use the script. I told you at the beginning of the rehearsals.

She moves to pick up the script.

BEN. What do you mean?

BARBARA. I haven't learnt it.

BEN. I'll feed you the lines.

BARBARA. I'd rather have the script.

BEN *picks up the script.*

BEN. His tears would not stop.

BARBARA. His tears would not stop.

BEN. He held my hand tight.

BARBARA. He held my hand tight.

BEN. Stop crying, the guard says.

BARBARA. Stop crying, the guard says.

BEN. But he couldn't.

BARBARA. But he couldn't.

BEN. Stop crying, the guard says.

BARBARA. Stop crying, the guard says.

BEN. Or I will shoot you.

BARBARA. Or I will shoot you.

BEN. But the boy could not.

BARBARA. But the boy could not.

BEN. His tears rolled out.

BARBARA. His tears rolled out.

BEN. So the guard walked up to them.

BARBARA. So the guard walked up to them.

BEN. He spoke quietly, matter of factly.

BARBARA. He spoke quietly, matter of factly.

BEN. If you do not stop crying.

BARBARA. If you do not stop crying.

BEN. I will kill you.

BARBARA. I will kill you.

BEN. Then his brother started to cry.

BARBARA. Then his brother started to cry.

BEN. Quiet tears.

BARBARA. Quiet tears.

BEN. Kneel down, said the guard.

BARBARA. Kneel down, said the guard.

BEN. Gently.

BARBARA. Gently.

BEN. And your brother.

BARBARA. And your brother.

BEN. The boys were confused.

BARBARA. The boys were confused.

BEN. Their lips were blue.

BARBARA. Their lips were blue.

BEN. The guard helped them.

BARBARA. The guard helped them.

BEN. He arranged them.

BARBARA. He arranged them.

BEN. So that the older boy was kneeling behind the younger one.

BARBARA. So that the older boy was kneeling behind the younger one.

BEN. He levelled their heads.

BARBARA. He levelled their heads.

BEN. So that they were at the same height.

BARBARA. So that they were at the same height.

BEN. He took out his gun.

BARBARA. He took out his gun.

> BARBARA *starts to cry quietly.*

> It's disrespectful.

BEN. It happened.

BARBARA. It was a long time ago.

BEN. For Eva it was yesterday, it was this morning, it was just now. For her whole life.

BARBARA. We all live on a pile of ash. It blows around us. Covers our faces. Makes us red-eyed and our mouths dry.

BEN. Kneel down, said the guard.

BARBARA. Kneel down, said the guard.

BEN. Quietly, gently.

BARBARA. Quietly, gently.

BEN. And your brother.

BARBARA. And your brother.

BEN. The boys were confused.

BARBARA. The boys were confused.

BEN. Their lips were blue.

BARBARA. Their lips were blue.

BEN. The guard helped them.

BARBARA. The guard helped them.

BEN. He arranged them.

BARBARA. He arranged them.

BEN. So that the older boy was kneeling . . .

BARBARA. So that the older boy was kneeling . . .

BEN. Behind the younger one.

BARBARA. Behind the younger one.

BEN. He levelled their heads.

BARBARA. He levelled their heads.

BEN. So that they were at the same height.

BARBARA. So that they were at the same height.

BEN. He was precise.

BARBARA. He was precise.

BEN. Then he shot them.

BARBARA. Then he shot them.

BEN. One bullet . . .

BARBARA. One bullet . . .

BEN. Through both their heads.

BARBARA. Through both their heads.

BEN. The guard said.

BARBARA. The guard said.

BEN. Why waste two bullets?

BARBARA. Why waste two bullets?

Silence.

EVA. Comfort me. Tell me kind things.

PETER. These things happened.

EVA. They happened to me. Not to you.

PETER. They're like salt. They've salted me. A few white crystals affecting everything.

EVA. Hold me.

PETER. You're safe now. Soon you'll be going home. The boys will meet you. There will be an allotment and you will dance quietly with them as the sun rises and the earth loses its dew.

EVA *dies.*

End.

A Nick Hern Book

Memory first published in Great Britain as a paperback original in 2006 by Nick Hern Books Limited, 14 Larden Road, London W3 7ST

Cover design: www.energydesignstudio.com

Typeset by Country Setting, Kingsdown, Kent CT14 8ES
Printed in Great Britain by Bookmarque, Croydon, Surrey

A CIP catalogue record for this book is available from the British Library

ISBN-10   1 85459 974 7
ISBN-13   978 1 85459 974 2